GOD'S WAY
TO
WHOLENESS

*Divine Healing by the
Power of the
Holy Spirit*

Jack W. Hayford
with
Nathaniel Van Cleave

THOMAS NELSON PUBLISHERS
Nashville

CONTENTS

God's Way to Wholeness: Divine Healing by the Power of the Holy Spirit is one of a series of study guides that focus exciting, discovery-geared coverage of Bible book and power themes—all prompting toward dynamic, Holy Spirit-filled living.

About the General Editor

JACK W. HAYFORD, noted pastor, teacher, writer, and composer, is the General Editor of the complete series, working with the publisher in the conceiving and developing of each of the books.

Dr. Hayford is Senior Pastor of The Church On The Way, the First Foursquare Church of Van Nuys, California. He and his wife, Anna, have four married children, all of whom are active in either pastoral ministry or vital church life. As General Editor of the *Spirit-Filled Life Bible,* Pastor Hayford led a four-year project, which has resulted in the availability of one of today's most practical and popular study Bibles. He is author of more than twenty books, including *A Passion for Fullness, The Beauty of Spiritual Language, Rebuilding the Real You,* and *Prayer Is Invading the Impossible.* His musical compositions number over four hundred songs, including the widely sung "Majesty."

About the Writer

NATHANIEL VAN CLEAVE is, at age 85, continuing an effective and fruitful public ministry that has been in progress for over sixty years. He and his wife, Lois, live in Southern California, where Dr. Van Cleave still conducts a speaking and teaching ministry that finds him a welcomed guest in scores of pulpits and a regular lecturer at LIFE Bible College and Calvary Chapel Bible College. He holds a Th.D. degree, having studied at LIFE Bible College, Los Angeles Baptist Theological Seminary, and the University of California.

As a lifetime member of the Foursquare Church clergy, Dr. Van Cleave has distinguished himself as a pastor, missionary, professor, and author *(Handbook on Preaching, Foundations of Pentecostal Theology* with G. P. Duffield, *The Vine and the Branches—A History of the International Church of the Foursquare Gospel).* Besides serving some of the most noted pastorates in his church fellowship, he has served in almost every office in the Foursquare movement except the presidency —supervisor, board member, general supervisor, and college president.

Of this contributor the General Editor has remarked:"Dr. Van Cleave's remarkable career of serving Christ as an instrument of blessing to so many in such versatile ways is a tribute to more than a man of great gifts. He is a man of great nobility of character, richness of thought, and brotherliness in relationships."

THE KEYS
THAT KEEP ON FREEING

Is there anything that holds more mystery or more genuine practicality than a key? The mystery: "What does it fit? What can it turn on? What might it open? What new discovery could be made? The practicality: Something *will* most certainly open to the possessor! Something *will* absolutely be found to unlock and allow a possibility otherwise obstructed!

- Keys describe the instruments we use to access or ignite.
- Keys describe the concepts that unleash mind-boggling possibilities.
- Keys describe the different structures of musical notes which allow variation and range.

Jesus spoke of keys: "And I will give you the keys of the kingdom of heaven, and whatever you bind on earth will be bound in heaven, and whatever you loose on earth will be loosed in heaven" (Matt. 16:19).

While there is no conclusive list of exactly what keys Jesus was referring to, it is clear that He did confer upon His church—upon *all* who believe—the access to a realm of spiritual partnership with Him in the dominion of His kingdom. Faithful students of the Word of God, moving in the practical grace and biblical wisdom of Holy Spirit-filled living and ministry, have noted some of the primary themes which undergird this order of "spiritual partnership" Christ offers. The "keys" are *concepts*—biblical themes that are traceable through the Scriptures and verifiably dynamic when applied with soundly based faith under the lordship of Jesus Christ. The "partnership" is the *essential* feature of this release of divine grace;

(1) believers reaching to *receive* Christ's promise of "kingdom keys," (2) while choosing to *believe* in the Holy Spirit's readiness to actuate their unleashing, unlimited power today.

Companioned with the Bible book studies in the *Spirit-Filled Life Study Guide* series, the Kingdom Dynamic studies present a dozen different themes. This study series is an outgrowth of the Kingdom Dynamics themes included throughout the *Spirit-Filled Life Bible,* which provide a treasury of insight developed by some of today's most respected Christian leaders. From that beginning, studious writers have evolved the elaborated studies you'll pursue here.

The central goal of the subjects focused on in this present series of study guides is to relate "power points" of the Holy Spirit-filled life. Assisting you in your discoveries are a number of helpful features. Each study guide has twelve to fourteen lessons, each arranged so you can plumb the depths or skim the surface, depending upon your needs and interests. The study guides contain major lesson features, each marked by a symbol and heading for easy identification.

WORD WEALTH

The WORD WEALTH feature provides important definitions of key terms.

BEHIND THE SCENES

BEHIND THE SCENES supplies information about cultural beliefs and practices, doctrinal disputes, business trades, and the like that illuminate Bible passages and teachings.

AT A GLANCE

The AT A GLANCE feature uses maps and charts to identify places and simplify themes or positions.

 KINGDOM EXTRA

Because this study guide focuses on a theme of the Bible, you will find a KINGDOM EXTRA feature that guides you into Bible dictionaries, Bible encyclopedias, and other resources that will enable you to glean more from the Bible's wealth on the topic if you want something extra.

 PROBING THE DEPTHS

Another feature, PROBING THE DEPTHS, will explain controversial issues raised by particular lessons and cite Bible passages and other sources to which you can turn to help you come to your own conclusions.

 FAITH ALIVE

Finally, each lesson contains a FAITH ALIVE feature. Here the focus is, So what? Given what the Bible says, what does it mean for my life? How can it impact my day-to-day needs, hurts, relationships, concerns, and whatever else is important to me? FAITH ALIVE will help you see and apply the practical relevance of God's literary gift.

As you'll see, these guides supply space for you to answer the study and life-application questions and exercises. You may, however, want to record all your answers, or just the overflow from your study or application, in a separate notebook or journal. This would be especially helpful if you think you'll dig into the KINGDOM EXTRA features. Because the exercises in this feature are optional and can be expanded as far as you want to take them, we have not allowed writing space for them in this study guide. So you may want to have a notebook or journal handy for recording your discoveries while working through to this feature's riches.

The Bible study method used in this series revolves around four basic steps: observation, interpretation, correlation, and application. Observation answers the question, What does the text say? Interpretation deals with, What does the text mean?—not with what it means to you or me, but what it meant to its original readers. Correlation asks, What light do other Scripture passages shed on this text? And application, the goal of Bible study, poses the question, How should my life change in response to the Holy Spirit's teaching of this text?

If you have used a Bible much before, you know that it comes in a variety of translations and paraphrases. Although you can use any of them with profit as you work through the *Spirit-Filled Life Kingdom Dynamics Study Guide* series, when Bible passages or words are cited, you will find they are from the New King James Version of the Bible. Using this translation with this series will make your study easier, but it's certainly not necessary.

The only resources you need to complete and apply these study guides are a heart and mind open to the Holy Spirit, a prayerful attitude, and a pencil and a Bible. Of course, you may draw upon other sources, such as commentaries, dictionaries, encyclopedias, atlases, and concordances, and you'll even find some optional exercises that will guide you into these sources. But these are extras, not necessities. These study guides are comprehensive enough to give you all you need to gain a good, basic understanding of the Bible book being covered and how you can apply its themes and counsel to your life.

A word of warning, though. By itself, Bible study will not transform your life. It will not give you power, peace, joy, comfort, hope, and a number of other gifts God longs for you to unwrap and enjoy. Through Bible study, you will grow in your understanding of the Lord, His kingdom and your place in it, and those things are essential. But you need more. You need to rely on the Holy Spirit to guide your study and your application of the Bible's truths. He, Jesus promised, was sent to teach us "all things" (John 14:26; cf. 1 Cor. 2:13). So as you use this series to guide you through Scripture, bathe your study time in prayer, asking the Spirit of God to illuminate the text, enlighten your mind, humble your will, and comfort your heart. He will never let you down.

My prayer and goal for you is that as you unlock and begin to explore God's Book for living His way, the Holy Spirit will fill every fiber of your being with the joy and power God longs to give all His children. So read on. Be diligent. Stay open and submissive to Him. You will not be disappointed. He promises you!

Lesson 1/Healing and God's Covenants

Some time ago, in a local church prayer service, one of the recent converts was heard to pray, "O God! Please do something; please do something!" The pastor did not interrupt the prayer, but after the service he counseled the young man, explaining, "Son, it isn't necessary to address God so indefinitely. He is a covenant-making and covenant-keeping God. You can ask for, and receive from the Lord, any one of His precious blessings and benefits revealed in His Holy Word. The Bible contains hundreds of such promises."

The dictionary defines a covenant as follows: "A formal, solemn, and binding contract between two or more parties especially for the performance of some action, or transfer of assets, usually modified by certain conditions." The Bible is actually a Covenant revealing what God will do for His people under what conditions. Many scholars prefer the terms Old and New Covenant to Old and New Testament. In fact, the Old Covenant contains several lesser covenants, some of which are conditional and some of which are unconditional. In Exodus 15:26 God makes a healing covenant with His people:

> If you diligently heed the voice of the LORD your God and do what is right in His sight, give ear to His commandments and keep all His statutes, I will put none of the diseases on you which I have brought on the Egyptians. For I *am* the LORD who heals you. (Read the whole context, vv. 22–27.)

In this passage, called the Old Testament Divine Healing Covenant, the Lord God not only makes a covenant to heal,

He reveals one of His names, "Yahweh Rapha." The Lord actually stated, "I am Yahweh Who Heals; this is My NAME." In the Old Testament (Covenant) we find at least nine compound names of Yahweh, each of which reveals a specific facet of God's nature. Other such compound names which reveal God's nature and covenant relationship are *Yahweh-Yireh*, "the Lord our Provider"; *Yahweh-Tsidkenu*, "the Lord our Righteousness"; *Yahweh-Raah*, "the Lord our Shepherd"; *Yahweh Shalom*, "The Lord our Peace"; and *Yahweh-Sabaoth*, "the Lord of Hosts." Whatever the Lord God is by nature— revealed by one of His stated names—He never ceases to be in relation to His people. From this covenant in Exodus 15 we know that the Lord will never cease to heal His people. We, of course, must take note that the promise is conditional. To receive the healing we must be obedient to His wishes.

Perhaps it would be helpful for us to examine the conditions on which divine healing is contingent, according to the Old Testament healing covenant; they are four:

1. Listen to the voice of the Lord.
2. Do what is right (righteous behavior) in His sight.
3. Give ear to God's commandments.
4. Keep all His statutes.

Make a brief elaboration in your own words of what each of those 4 conditions says and how each might apply to you today.

1.

2.

3.

4.

The last two conditions actually merge into one: "Listen to and keep all God's commandments or statutes." That *commandments* and *statutes* are synonyms can be seen, for example, in verses 105–112 from Psalm 119, which is a Psalm about knowing and living by God's holy Word. In those verses, *word, judgments, law, precepts,* and *statutes* are synonymous terms having reference to God's revealed will by which His people will order their lives. It is clear that the psalmist was praying for both physical and spiritual healing (see v. 107). As he sought God, he vowed to walk by God's Word and keep His statutes in exact conformity with the Old Testament healing covenant.

For New Testament believers, fulfilling the conditions of the healing covenant means living our lives according to the Word of God. If we desire to have strong faith for divine healing we need to hide God's Word in our hearts, and with the help of the Holy Spirit walk according to scriptural guidance.

WORD WEALTH

Heals, *rapha'.* To cure, heal, repair, mend, restore health. Its participial form *rophe',* "one who heals," is the Hebrew word for doctor. The main idea of the verb *rapha'* is physical healing. Some have tried to explain away the biblical teaching of divine healing, but all can see that this verse speaks of physical diseases and their divine cure. The first mention of *rapha'* in the Bible (Gen. 20:17) refers unquestionably to the cure of a physical condition, as do references to healing from leprosy and boils (Lev. 13:18; 14:3). Scripture affirms, "I am Yahweh your physician."[1]

Who prayed to God for the healing of another in Genesis 20:17?

What was the result of the above prayer?

For what does the writer (David) pray in Psalm 6? What was the result?

How does God answer prayer for the psalmist in Psalm 30? (v. 3)

     BEHIND THE SCENES

The healing covenant promise given in Exodus 15:26 is given in connection with historical events in which God has taught us important spiritual lessons. After the crossing of the Red Sea in flight from Egypt and their great rejoicing over their miracle deliverance from Pharaoh, the children of Israel came to the dry desert wilderness. They traveled for three days without water. They finally arrived at an oasis called Marah. There was water at Marah, but it was so bitter they couldn't drink it. The people began to complain against Moses and against the Lord. When Moses, the intercessor, cried out to God, He showed him a healing tree whose branches, when cast into the bitter waters, sweetened the water. God's revealed remedy healed the bitterness.

The waters of Marah typify the bitter experiences of life, some of which are sicknesses. Sometimes sickness is a testing experience in which God teaches us a lesson of faith and patience. When we cry out to God, He supplies the branches of healing that turn bitter water to sweet.

Not only did the Lord heal the bitter waters, He led them to Elim, where there were twelve wells of water and seventy palm trees for their encampment. God led His people from the Red Sea to Marah to Elim. God so orders that all things work *together* for good. If your Marah is a sickness, *Yahweh-Rapha* may well have an Elim awaiting you.

What was the sin of the people when they complained against Moses? (Rom. 14:23)

What ought the people to have done instead of grumbling?

Can you think of any current example of human bitterness or complaint, and how that might hinder God's flow of healing grace?

Another of the Lord's covenants, called the New Testament Healing Covenant, is found in James 5:13–16. (Read this passage.) The human author of the Book of James, from which the New Testament healing covenant is taken, was James, the brother of the Lord Jesus. After the martyrdom of James the brother of John, James the brother of Jesus became the leader of the apostolic church (Acts 15; Mark 6:3). Being the brother of the Lord and the leading apostle, he certainly understood the Lord's plan for the people of the Christian church. It is not likely that James, writing under the inspiration of the Holy Spirit, would have prescribed prayers by "elders" as a remedy for the sick and afflicted of the church if divine healing was soon to be abandoned along with everything miraculous, as some teachers contend.

James does not say that prayer by elders is the only remedy for sickness. Actually, all real healing comes directly or indirectly from God. No medicine would cure sickness unless God had created man with built-in healing characteristics. What James says is that prayer should be the believers' first recourse when they are sick. The discoveries and applications of nature's therapeutic substances, such as antibiotics, were no doubt in the Creator's forethought. The believers are in no way deprived of precise surgical skills. However, for believers, praying for God's healing power applied by the blessed Holy

Spirit is their first step toward wholeness. There is no conscientious physician who would not welcome prayer as a remedy along with his medicines and procedures.

What benefit is there for a Christian to experience direct healing in answer to prayer?

What benefit comes to the local church when sick members are healed in answer to the prayer of faith by the elders?

Is there not a special blessing for the church when a member has a remarkable recovery from sickness or surgery and united prayer has preceded the surgical or medical procedure?

Let's take a look at several aspects of the healing covenant as set forth by James.

1. When sickness comes, pray. "Is anyone among you suffering? let him <u>pray</u>." Paul wrote to the Thessalonians: "Rejoice always, pray without ceasing, in everything give thanks; for this is the will of God in Christ Jesus for you" (1 Thess. 5:16–18). If we have developed the habit of regular, systematic prayer, then prayer will be a natural reaction to everything that happens. Someone will ask, "What if a sudden emergency develops? Shouldn't the first step be to call 911?" Perhaps, but one can pray all the way to the phone. Jesus tells us that we are not heard for our much speaking; if someone else makes the 911 call, pray all the way to the emergency room.

2. Next, James addresses people who are not sick: "Is anyone cheerful? Let him sing psalms." How are we to take this admonition inserted into the midst of teaching about healing for the sick? There are two ways, at least, that this may be taken.

First, if people were joyful in spirit, with a song in their hearts, they undoubtedly would have better health and be sick less. Counselors are quite agreed that a positive attitude is an aid to good health, and that a negative frame of mind, from which come fear, worry, anger, suspicion, and strife, brings on many kinds of illness.

It can also be taken that the joyful hymn singing of the healthy members can do much to strengthen the faith of the weak members, giving them a positive upward look. Sick people are likely to become discouraged. Joyful praise in song can lift spirits. There is something in the idea of a collective psychology. However, the cheerful singers may be those whom God has already healed of afflictions. Their joyful singing could help the sick members to believe more strongly in the healing power of the Holy Spirit.

Describe an experience of having your faith lifted by being among joyful, singing people?

Can you remember ever being depressed by being in the midst of joyless people?

3. Call for the elders of the church. Some sick people seem to think the verse instructs them to "wish for the elders of the church." They tell no one of their plight; and, when no one calls to visit them, they feel slighted and sometimes criticize the pastor and the church for neglecting them. The covenant here in James 5 places the responsibility on the sick person to call for the elders, or to have someone call on their behalf. On the other hand, it does not say that the sick person must go looking for the elders. The original Greek word for "call" means "bid [the elders] to come." The elders James had in mind made house calls. However, if the sick person is able to attend the church service, it is reasonable that he or she should ask for prayer by the elders during or at the end of the service. It appears, though, that every church should have available to visit the sick those who have a gift of the Spirit or who are people in whose faith the sick have confidence to pray for healing. The modern equivalent of "elders" could be the

"pastors," "assisting pastors," "lay elders," "deacons," "visiting committee," and so on; however, such should be able to pray the prayer of faith.

WORD WEALTH

Elder, *presbuteros*. "An old man, elder, one more advanced in age, or experienced to lead." In the Jewish synagogue the leader was called an elder. The church followed the same nomenclature (Luke 7:3). Peter called himself an elder (1 Pet. 5:1). Paul summoned the elders of the church at Ephesus for a final charge (Acts 20:17), and, in verse 28, Paul referred to the elders as overseers, which was the job description of elders who were to shepherd the flock. In Titus 1:5–7, Paul admonishes Titus to appoint elders in every church in Crete; then, in verse 7, he calls them *bishops,* or those who were to oversee the church. An elder, then, was one who was the *overseer/bishop* of the affairs of the church. Paul, in 1 Timothy 5:17, calls upon Timothy to give honor to the elders, and special honor to those who ministered the Word. Apparently there were teaching elders and ruling elders. There were usually several elders in the average church, with many in the larger churches. Since the church in Bible times, under Roman rule, could not build sanctuaries, they often met in houses of the members (Rom. 16:5) with an elder over each house group; when the whole body met together there would be a plurality of elders.

The relationship of spiritual gifts to the healing ministry of the "elder" deserves discussion. The Book of James in which we find the New Testament healing covenant makes no mention of the spiritual gifts discussed in 1 Corinthians 12. At least three of the spiritual gifts of 1 Corinthians are related to divine healing. The first is called "the gifts of healings." The fact that *gifts* and *healings* are both plural suggests that the gift is for the whole church, not to any individual. The plurality of the term "gifts" could indicate that each case of healing is a gift which God bestows through a spiritual church. The Bible makes no mention of a "gift to heal," and practically no one makes claim to such a gift.

Another *charisma* is termed the gift of "faith." Since all faith is a gift from God, this gift is usually called by Bible scholars "the gift of special faith." The gift is probably seen in action in Acts 3:2–9 and Acts 14:8–15 where both Peter and Paul prayed for, and brought deliverance to men lame from birth. In both cases the apostles commanded the lame men to rise and walk.

Paul in 1 Corinthians 12 lists another gift called "working of miracles." Again, the plural form suggests that the gift belonged to the church rather than to any individual. Some feel that this gift applied not so much to healings as to other types of miracles, such as the raising of Dorcas from the dead (Acts 9:39–42).

Sometimes the gift of a "word of knowledge" is said to describe the capacity to reveal that certain persons are suffering from a certain type of sickness; there are no clear biblical examples of this particular operation, and many scholars believe that the gift of the "word of knowledge" is intended for the ministry of the teacher.

Make a quick overview of Acts. How many healing miracles can you readily identify in that book? Can you note any healing accounts in the Book of Acts that might be an example of calling for the elders of the church? (Could 9:36–43 be a case of such?)

4. The Catholic church tradition has called the passage in James 5:13–15 the sacrament of "extreme unction," making it the basis for the anointing of one who is at the point of death. Pentecostals and charismatics can see in the passage justification for a sacrament of divine healing, but death was far from present in the mind of James, for he says of the sick that "the Lord will raise him up."

Can you find in James 5:13–18 three clearly positive results of prayer?

1.

2.

3.

5. What is the meaning and purpose for the anointing with oil? There are some Bible teachers who see in the oil a medicinal remedy and who contend that oil was often used in Bible times for medicinal purposes. That the word was used in a symbolic anointing is clearly seen in Mark 6:12, 13. In whatever way people of Bible times may have used olive oil, James states that the "prayer of faith will save the sick," not the application of olive oil. Furthermore, if we believe that the Scriptures are Holy Spirit-inspired, we cannot believe that the Lord would recommend an oil massage as the remedy for every kind of sickness.

The oil was used as a symbol of the work of the Holy Spirit. Its application declared that the healing was a result of the work of the Spirit of God, not the power and holiness of the elders who prayed (Acts 3:11–16). James, speaking under inspiration of the Holy Spirit, said concerning the results of the prayer and anointing, "the Lord will raise him [the sick] up." Jesus anointed a blind man's eyes with clay and sent him to wash away the clay in the Pool of Siloam; the blind man obeyed and received his sight (John 9:6–12). No one will suppose that the clay was a medicinal remedy for blindness. The use of the clay was as the anointing with oil in James 5, a symbol and act of obedience. By no means are we saying that the use of proven remedies is wrong for a Christian, but in the case of the healing covenant no curative property of oil is intended.

PROBING THE DEPTHS

"And the Lord will raise him up" clarifies the true source of the restoration. James thus excludes the idea that the anointing oil possesses any magical qualities. "The Lord" is again best understood as denoting the Lord Jesus Christ, the one in whose name the anointing was done. As the Lord over the lives of His people, He heals according to His will. "Will raise him up" virtually repeats "will save" earlier in the verse, meaning that the sick person will be raised up from his sickbed.[2]

What reasons can you suggest the Holy Spirit may have for the act of anointing with oil along with prayer for the sick?

6. Several avenues to divine healing are mentioned in the passage in James 5.

a) The sick person can pray for himself or herself (v. 13). Many healings are the result of sick persons praying for themselves. One may be in a place where there are no available elders or other persons to help in prayer.

b) In verse 16 believers are commanded to pray one for another in order that they might be healed. This is called intercessory prayer and is a high form of supplication. Many persons have testified to having been healed as a result of forgetting self to intercede for another.

Jesus taught, "Again I say to you that if two of you agree on earth concerning anything that they ask, it will be done for them by My Father in heaven" (Matt. 18:19).

c) Verse 16 also suggests that one might seek out someone like Elijah who is known to have great faith, adding, "The effective, fervent prayer of a righteous man avails much." All believers are righteous in the righteousness of Christ; those who believe are justified; however, some persons devote much time to prayer, the Word of God, and to walking in the Holy Spirit. Elijah had his weaknesses, but he was a man of faith who walked with God. In every church there may be several, besides the pastors (elders), who humbly walk with God, who pray the prayer of faith.

Whom do you know in your church to whom you might go for the prayer of faith?

Have you ever called for the elders or someone in whom you have confidence to pray for you in a time of sickness or suffering? Review what happened.

7. In 5:16, James suggests that believers confess their trespasses to one another as an avenue to bodily healing. This is not always easy, for one cannot always find someone mature enough to be a reliable auditor of confession. It may be that James has in mind here confessions where there are offenses. If we have offended someone or been offended by another person, prayer for healing, or for any other need may be futile until we have forgiven and been forgiven. If we cannot find someone to whom we may make a confession of sin or transgression, we certainly do well to confess to the Lord. It may be that the only barrier to complete healing may be unconfessed sin of envy, jealousy, hatred, or slight.

Have you ever confessed an offense to another, or had another person confess to you? What happened?

Have you any area of life that needs this discipline now?

FAITH ALIVE

Quite clearly, divine healing is one of the blessings which the Lord has provided for His people. We learned that one of the Lord's names is *Yahweh-Rapha,* "the Lord our Healer." We saw that what the Lord reveals about His nature, He will always be to His people. When Jesus the Redeemer came in the fullness of time, He spent much of His earthly ministry healing the sick, not only to demonstrate His deity, but because He was moved with compassion, seeing people as wounded sheep without a shepherd.

Jesus sent His followers forth, commanding them to "heal the sick" (Matt. 10:8). In His Great Commission, He promised His disciples that signs would follow their preaching and teaching—that they would lay hands on the sick and the sick would be healed. James, the brother of Jesus and the leader of the apostolic church wrote, inspired by the Holy Spirit, "Is anyone among you sick? Let him call for the elders of the church, and let them pray over him, anointing him with oil in the name of the Lord. And the prayer of faith will save the sick, and the Lord will raise him up. And if he has committed sins, he will be forgiven."

Since these provisions have been made for Christian believers, it is our privilege to receive divine healing in answer to prayer. It is our divinely ordained prerogative to seek healing through the channel of prayer—prayer by another believer or prayer by the elders of the church. If we lack faith, we can pray for faith. This is not to say that we will be remiss if we resort to medical remedies or surgical procedures. However, there is no blessing much more fulfilling than to experience the power of God healing our physical bodies. Even if we resort to remedies, we have the avenue of prayer that God will energize the medicine or the practitioner. We might be surprised to know how miraculously God can and is willing to work in us if we put our full confidence in His great and loving power. "Is anyone among you suffering? Let him <u>pray</u>."

---

1. *Spirit-Filled Life Bible* (Nashville, TN: Thomas Nelson Publishers, 1991), 105, "Word Wealth: 15:26 heals."

2. D. Edmond Hiebert, *The Epistle of James* (Chicago, IL: Moody Press, 1979).

Lesson 2/Healing and the Cross

The cross of Christ, together with His resurrection, is at the very heart of Christianity; it is the very center of the gospel message. On the cross sin and sickness lost their sting. When we look away to the cross, we see Jesus with the wounds in His hands, feet, and side; a second look reveals an open tomb, and we know that the long-typified redemption from the curse of sin is "finished"; our hope swells beyond the clouds when we see Jesus *lifted up for us*. "By His stripes we are healed" (Is. 53:5).

HEALING AND THE BRONZE SERPENT LIFTED UP

In the time of Moses, God provided a graphic symbol for the healing power of the Cross (see Num. 21:5–9). The sinning people had provoked the Lord with their continual accusations against Moses and even against the Lord God. Their sinful, adamic natures were out of control; Eden's curse was in full manifestation. God had provided daily manna, but they loathed the very taste of it, belittling God's gracious provision. They went so far as to transfer their loathing to God and to His appointed leader. Their sinful outbursts of strife and contention stalled the long hoped for journey to the Promised Land. Their rebellious act and attitude brought horrible affliction upon their entire encampment; multitudes fell to the bite and sting of "fiery serpents." Death appeared to rule. However, as always, God graciously provided a healing remedy. At God's command Moses lifted up a bronze serpent on a pole with the promise that all who looked away in faith to the brazen serpent would be restored. There was life for a look, grace in a glance, victory in a vision of God's redeeming emblem of sin judged and expiated.

BEHIND THE SCENES

The Focus of Divine Healing. The plague of fiery serpents, sent upon God's people was, in reality, a self-inflicted punishment, resulting from their frequent murmuring. God's judgment was in allowing what their own presumption invited, and many died from the bites of the serpents. But in answer to the repentance of His people, God prescribed the erecting of a bronze serpent to which any might look in faith and be healed. Jesus referred to this account in John 3:14, 15. Jesus clearly implied that the bronze serpent typified His being raised upon the Cross. Our healing, both spiritual and physical, comes from looking to and identifying with Christ crucified, "by whose stripes you were healed" (1 Pet. 2:24).[1]

HEALING AND THE LAMB OF GOD LIFTED UP

We clearly see from the passage in Numbers 21 that two distinct remedies and benefits came from looking away to the uplifted emblem of Christ crucified. The blessings were the forgiveness of their sins and the healing of their afflicted bodies. The gracious benefits were twofold: first, spiritual, in the cleansing of their sin-besmirched souls, and second, physical, in the healing of the venomous bites. The lifeline that is cast out from the Cross to a sinful and afflicted humanity has two saving strands: salvation of the soul and healing for the body. That we are interpreting rightly the words of Jesus is made clear in the very central scripture passage of the New Testament—John 3:14–17.

The word *saved* in verse 17 of that passage has reference to a full salvation, to a redemption that includes the total person. When Jesus said, "For God did not send His Son into the world to condemn the world, but that the world through Him might be <u>saved</u>," He meant by the term *saved* the salvation of the whole person, body and soul. That the word for saved means both physical and spiritual salvation is seen in the "Word Wealth" box that follows.

WORD WEALTH

Saved, *sozo.* To save, cure, heal, preserve, keep safe and sound, rescue from danger or destruction, deliver, to save from peril, injury or suffering, to make whole from physical death by healing, and from spiritual death by forgiving sin and its effects.[2] The word *sozo* is used 16 times in the New Testament to mean bodily healing. The passages are the following: Matt. 9:21, 22; Mark 5:23, 28, 34; 6:56; 10:52; Luke 7:50; 8:36, 48, 50; 17:19; 18:42; Acts 4:9; 14:9; James 5:15.

AN EXPIRED REMEDY FOR HEALING LIFTED UP

A word of caution needs to be given as we consider the bronze serpent that Moses lifted up in the wilderness. He did this at God's command in order to bring healing to the sick and dying Israelites. The bronze serpent on a pole was a symbol pointing ahead to the fullness of time when Jesus, the promised Redeemer, would come to fulfill all the types, shadows, and symbols of the Old Testament. When Jesus was lifted up on the Cross, He fulfilled the bronze serpent typology. Now we need only to exercise faith in the finished work of the Cross.

In 2 Kings 18:3, 4 mention is made of an evil practice of "bronze serpent" worship, which the good King Hezekiah abolished. The bronze serpent was given once only as a sign of the people's sin being judged and expiated; it was not intended as an object of worship. It pointed ahead to the vicarious atoning death of Christ on a Cross where all sin was being judged. Christ's once-and-for-all sacrifice was never intended to be repeated; it was a finished work. We honor the memory, not of the Cross itself, which was an atrocious instrument of capital punishment, but the Sacrifice that was offered there for our salvation. It is not the Cross itself that saves us, but faith in Christ and His atoning work.

If we look to a cross-shaped physical object or to any kind of amulet to obtain healing or forgiveness, we are perpetuating an abuse like the worship of the bronze serpent, which King Hezekiah abolished. There may be some persons who can employ the objects only to remind them of the events and the spiritual realities; but at some point, invariably, objects of recall become objects of worship. Some may avoid the abuse, yet, as role models, they lead others less knowledgeable to an act of idolatry.

Furthermore, if we look only to the Cross, we have gone only halfway, because the complete work of full salvation for body and soul must include the empty tomb, the glorious Resurrection. Christ not only died, He arose and is seated at the right hand of God to be our Intercessor and High Priest. The work of the Cross purchased our salvation, but the broad stream of its glorious benefits flows from the mercy seat at the throne of grace. The Savior whom we worship is a living Christ who is the same yesterday, today, and forever.

Note any contemporary instances you have heard or know of, where superstition has focused on objects for seeking God's goodness.

Write your thoughts as to how this same thing may be done when people look to some anointed minister for healing.

GOD'S HEALING AND REDEEMING MAGNET LIFTED UP

For another passage of scripture that makes reference to the "lifting up" of Jesus, read John 8:26–30. The world, including Jesus' own disciples, did not really *know* Him as the Savior and Redeemer until He died and rose again. They knew Him as the great teacher, and even as the promised Messiah who would reign over a coming kingdom. But only the Cross revealed Him as the suffering Lamb of God who would take away the sins and afflictions of the world, in spite of the fact that John the Baptist had presented Him as such.

WORD WEALTH

Know, *ginosko.* Compare "prognosis," "gnomic," "gnostic." To perceive, understand, recognize, gain knowledge, realize, come to know. *Ginosko* is the knowledge that has an inception, a progress, and an attainment. It is the recognition of truth by personal experience.[3]

Since the Lord Jesus Christ died on the cross for our sins and afflictions, millions have come to know Him as their Savior and Healer.

And He died for all, that those who live should live no longer for themselves, but for Him who died for them and rose again. Therefore, from now on, we regard no one according to the flesh. Even though we have known Christ according to the flesh, yet now we know *Him thus* no longer. Therefore, if anyone *is* in Christ, *he is* a new creation; old things have passed away; behold, all things have become new" (2 Cor. 5:15–17).

We know Him in the Spirit.

PROBING THE DEPTHS

There is yet another scripture passage that pinpoints Christ's being lifted up on the cross: John 12:20–33. Read this passage and lift from it (writing below) three timeless slogans that characterize and summarize Jesus' ministry.

1.

2.

3.

There is perhaps not a greater passage in the New Testament than this in John 12. The Greeks sought Jesus; perhaps they came to invite Jesus to bring His teachings to Greece; possibly they were like the Macedonian (Greek) man in Acts 16 who in Paul's vision invited him to come over to help them. John's Greeks came too soon; they came before the Cross.

Jesus explained that the hour of His glorification was at hand. What other men would have called their hour of ignominy their hour of glory? Jesus called it the hour in which He would be glorified. He was not oblivious to the awful bitterness of the cup of Calvary's suffering. The thought crossed His mind that the Father could save Him from the Cross's awful ordeal of sin bearing and the grave's seeming defeat. But then came the willing surrender to the Father's will, and the words flowed out in exultation, "But for this purpose I came to this hour." He came to be planted; He declared that to have a harvest of redemption the seed of provision had to fall into the ground, but the planted grain of wheat would bring forth a worldwide ingathering of souls saved to the uttermost.

Then, Jesus cried out, "I, if I am lifted up from the earth, will draw all *peoples* to Myself." He could envision multitudes of the sick and the guilty dropping their crushing burdens at the foot of the cross. No wonder that He said that the hour of His glory had come! Paul, in Philippians 2:5–11, expressed the humiliation and the exaltation perfectly. For further enrichment, read this passage.

AN EFFECTIVE PRAYER FOR HEALING LIFTED UP

There are times when the Lord's redeemed followers enter into the fellowship of His sufferings and thereby become more dedicated and effective servants. The apostles of Jesus, in their endeavor to spread the good news of the full salvation that emanated from the Cross and the empty tomb, suffered severe persecution. They especially suffered in their attempt to preach the good news of the Resurrection. They were imprisoned and threatened with even greater punishment if they continued to preach publicly the resurrection of Jesus. The apostles gathered together to report the threats. They refreshed their minds about Christ's purpose in coming to earth and about the meaning of His cross and resurrection. Then they united in the following prayer:

> Now, Lord, look on their threats, and grant to Your servants that with all *boldness* they may speak Your word, by stretching out Your hand to heal, and that signs and wonders may be done through the name of Your holy Servant Jesus. And when they had prayed, the place where they were assembled together was shaken; and they were all filled with the Holy Spirit, and they spoke the word of God with boldness.
>
> (Acts 4:29–31)

The disciples said, in effect, "Lord we know what a complete salvation Christ, Your Son, purchased with His atoning death on the cross. We saw that a great victory came for Your gospel through the healing of the lame man; now we have been forbidden to preach the Resurrection in Jerusalem; Lord, stretch forth Your hand to heal the sick and thereby grant us new boldness to preach the truth in spite of all threatenings." The Lord answered, sending them a private spiritual earthquake and with it a new Pentecost and a renewed *boldness*. Afterward God gave great healing miracles through Peter, Philip, and Stephen.

> And through the hands of the apostles many signs and wonders were done among the people. And they were all with one accord in Solomon's Porch. Yet none of the rest dared join them, but the people esteemed them highly. And believers were increasingly added to the Lord, multitudes of both men and women, so that they brought the sick out into the streets and laid *them* on beds and couches, that at least the shadow of Peter passing by might fall on some of them. Also a multitude gathered from the surrounding cities to Jerusalem, bringing sick people and those who were tormented by unclean spirits, and they were all healed. (Acts 5:12–16)

The bold proclamation of the resurrection of Jesus from the grave, together with the teaching that the Lord was a living Savior and Healer, drew multitudes into the kingdom of Christ.

 WORD WEALTH

Boldness, *parrhesia.* Outspokenness, unreserved utterance, freedom of speech, with frankness, candor, cheerful courage, and the opposite of cowardice, timidity, or fear. Here it denotes a divine enablement that comes to ordinary and unprofessional people exhibiting spiritual power and authority. It also refers to a clear presentation of the gospel without being ambiguous or unintelligible. *Parrhesia* is not a human quality but a result of being filled with the Holy Spirit.[4]

God gave boldness to His disciples because they desired above all thoughts of self-preservation to see the gospel of full salvation bring redemption and healing to the countless multitudes of sick and guilt-stricken people. It seems that similar results are happening today where God's people are praying for boldness through the power of the Spirit of God.

A CRY FOR HEALING MERCY LIFTED UP

A very interesting miracle story is that of the healing of blind Bartimaeus, which you can read in Luke 18:31–43.

On Jesus' last journey to Jerusalem, just before they reached Jericho, He explained to His disciples that He would be betrayed, insulted, and crucified, but that He would rise from the dead on the third day. The disciples were bewildered by His prophecy of death; in fact, the prediction was beyond their comprehension. After all the teaching of their Master, they could not get beyond the prevalent hope that He had come to set up an earthly kingdom. There was no way they could fit death into the picture. A Cross was unthinkable.

Surprisingly, they were about to encounter a blind beggar who would have a clearer concept of the mission of Jesus than any of them. When blind Bartimaeus heard that Jesus of

Nazareth was passing through Jericho, he uttered a frantic cry, "Son of David, have <u>mercy</u> on me!" This he repeated twice against the protest of Jesus' disciples. One has to ask the question, "How in the world did this blind roadside beggar know that Jesus of Nazareth was the heir to David's messianic throne? How did he know about the "sure mercies of David" (Is. 53:3)? Since "Son of David" was one of the names of the Messiah, he might have picked the name up from some roadside conversation, but how did he associate the prophecies about the *sure mercies of David* with Jesus, so that he could claim mercy from Him in the form of healing for his blind-from-birth eyes? We have to believe that God somehow revealed it to him, as He had earlier revealed to the centurion that Jesus could heal from a distance by just the speaking of a word. To trace the conjoined theme of "David" and "mercy," see the following texts: Psalm 89:20–24; Isaiah 55:3, 4; and Acts 13:32–38.

Bartimaeus did not know about Jesus' prophecy to His disciples of His imminent death and resurrection. He had no concept, that we know, of Christ's atoning death and resurrection, but he knew what both the psalmist and the prophet Isaiah foretold—namely, that He who would be the Messiah (Son of David) would have "sure mercies" to dispense. He knew well that David had long ago died and had seen corruption, but he seemed to sense that the Son of David (Messiah) would have the power and *mercy* to open his blind eyes.

According to Paul's sermon in Acts 13, the Son of David would be raised from the dead and the risen Christ would bestow the sure mercies of David. Among those mercies would be forgiveness of sins and the healing of the sick, both of which blessings would be manifested in Paul's ministry in Iconium and Lystra.

In what areas do you most want to see God's healing power exhibited?

FAITH ALIVE

We may be sure that He who died for our sins and was raised for our justification still today bestows upon those who believe both full salvation for the soul and full healing for the sick. He who was lifted up on a cross to die for our sin and guilt conquered death and judgment for all believers. His triumph included the experience of all the "sure mercies" of David. The "sure mercies" are benefits of the kingdom in which the Lamb of God has already become, spiritually, the Lion of the Tribe of Judah. If you are afflicted, cry out in faith, "Son of David, have mercy!" He will answer, "Your faith has made you well."

1. *Spirit-Filled Life Bible* (Nashville, TN: Thomas Nelson Publishers, 1991), 226, "Kingdom Dynamics: The Focus of Divine Healing."
2. Ibid., 1525, "Word Wealth: 7:50 saved."
3. Ibid., 1589, "Word Wealth: 8:32 know."
4. Ibid., 1632, "Word Wealth: 4:31 boldness."

Lesson 3/Healing and Repentance

What is repentance?

We usually think of repentance as applied to sinners coming to Christ for the first time. After Peter's sermon on the day of Pentecost, the people cried out under great conviction of sin, "Men *and* brethren, what shall we do? Peter answered as follows: "Repent, and let every one of you be baptized in the name of Jesus Christ for the remission of sins; and you shall receive the gift of the Holy Spirit" (Acts 2:38). A few days later Peter spoke to a crowd of inquiring sinners, explaining: "Repent therefore and be converted, that your sins may be blotted out" (Acts 3:19). When Jesus came preaching the gospel of the kingdom, He said, "The time is fulfilled, and the kingdom of God is at hand. Repent, and believe in the gospel" (Mark 1:15).

Nevertheless, disobedient, careless, sinning Christians are also called to repentance. Paul called upon the morally delinquent members of the church in Corinth to repent of their ways, for the fornication and lewdness of which they were guilty (2 Cor. 12:20, 21). Likewise, when John, at the dictation of Jesus, wrote to the seven churches of Asia, the letter to the people of the church at Ephesus (the best of the seven churches) concluded with the warning to repent "or else I will come to you quickly and remove your lampstand from its place" (Rev. 2:5).

WORD WEALTH

Repent, *metanoeo.* From *meta,* "after," and *noeo* "to think." Repentance is a decision that results in a change of mind, which in turn leads to a change of purpose and action.[1]

PROBING THE DEPTHS

Our concept of "repentance" is often equated to "emotional sorrow and regret." However the biblical words (*sub* in Hebrew, and *metanoeo* in Greek) have the meaning of "change of mind and direction," to do an "about-face." Sorrow and regret often accompany repentance—in fact, remorse is a very important prelude to repentance—but simply to say "I'm sorry" is more times than not a sorrow for the consequences of sin, not for the act of sin. Paul states in 2 Corinthians 7:9, 10, "Now I rejoice, not that you were made sorry, but that your sorrow led to repentance. . . . For <u>godly</u> <u>sorrow</u> <u>produces</u> <u>repentance</u> *leading* to salvation, not to be regretted; but the sorrow of the world produces death."

If sorrow and regret lead to repentance, the repentance obviously is something beyond the sorrow or remorse. If we are genuinely sorry and regretful of our wrongdoing, we will change directions in our conduct and change attitude in our purpose. Both Judas Iscariot and Simon the sorcerer experienced excruciating sorrow, but neither sincerely turned to God. The Lord is not deceived by crocodile tears. The Lord responds to the change in our central resolve that turns us from self to the divine will for our lives.

Repentance is a change in what? Describe an instance of your own repenting.

What is the difference between remorse over sin and repentance?

Can you think of three biblical instances, of sorrow (either false or genuine) being expressed for sin?

What did Paul say was the relationship between godly sorrow and true repentance?

Christians sometimes sin, as John said in his first epistle: "If we say that we have no sin, we deceive ourselves, and the truth is not in us. If we confess our sins, He is faithful and just to forgive us *our* sins and to cleanse us from all unrighteousness" (1 John 1:8, 9). Genuine believers do not live in and practice overt sins; if they do, they have become apostate (1 John 3:7–9). However, Christians often commit sins of attitude, sins of omission, sins of neglect, sins of unbelief and sins of disposition, and so on. The writer of Hebrews says, "whom the LORD loves He chastens" (Heb. 12:6). Sometimes that chastening comes in the form of sickness; however, let me say at once that all sickness is not the result of any sin or sins (John 9:1–3). If a sickness is a form of the Lord's chastening, repentance will have to happen before healing will come. In the New Testament healing covenant of James 5:13–16, it is clear that confession of sin and repentance are, in many cases, necessary before the elders, or praying persons, can pray the prayer of faith for the sick one.

There are several Bible passages that deal with the relationship between delay in answered prayer for healing and a change in attitude and conduct. These *repentance* passages we will examine in this chapter.

THE CASE OF MIRIAM'S LEPROSY (Numbers 12:1–15)

Numbers 12:1–15 records not only the healing of Miriam from leprosy, but also the sad story of her misconduct, which led to her grievous affliction. This spiritually gifted woman permitted herself to become guilty of at least seven sins, six of which were sins of attitude. Before we study them, see how many you can identify as you read and meditate on this passage. Her sins were as follows:

1. The Sin of Rebellion and Wrongful Criticism

Miriam (the sister of Moses) and her brother Aaron bitterly criticized Moses for his marriage to Zipporah, the daughter of Jethro, because she was a Cushite and probably of a different color, although this is not certain. We know that Jethro's family was a godly family. The Cushites were not among those with whom the Israelites were forbidden to marry. Actually, Miriam and Aaron were rebelling against the authority of Moses, using his wife as an excuse or cover for their real motive. We certainly have the right to offer suggestions to spiritual leaders, but to criticize them actually does harm to both parties.

2. The Sin of Jealousy and Envy

Miriam's criticism of Moses' wife was only a cover for jealousy. When Moses' work of judging the people became more than he could handle, Jethro, his father-in-law, suggested that he choose seventy elders to help him with his overwhelming task of judging the needs and grievances of more than one-half million people (see Num. 11:21–30; Ex. 18:1–27). There is no doubt that Aaron and Miriam were spiritually gifted persons; Aaron was the first high priest; Miriam is called a prophetess; she had composed a song in the Spirit; she was the leader of the women of Israel (Ex. 15:20, 21). But having a gift of the Spirit does not qualify one to make demands of leadership. Miriam was guilty of *jealousy.*

3. The Sin of Racial Prejudice

While Miriam's real motive was that of jealousy, she was prejudiced or she would not have referred to the race and possibly the color of Moses' wife. Moses' wife's father had given Moses the advice from which he had reorganized the leadership structure of the nation. Aaron and Miriam, Moses' relatives, were envious and jealous because they were not consulted about the appointment of elders. To hide their real motives they drummed up racial criticism of Moses for marrying Zipporah, the daughter of Jethro. At the same time Miriam uncovered her racial prejudice.

4. The Sin of Inordinate Pride

That Miriam was guilty of spiritual pride is seen clearly in verse 2: "So they said, 'Has the LORD indeed spoken only through Moses? Has He not spoken through us also?' And the LORD heard it." Yes, God had spoken through Aaron and Miriam; they were valuable servants of the Lord. We must remember, however, that God will at any time speak through whomever He wishes to use as a channel. No one for being used once establishes any claim on God's management of His affairs.

5. The Sin of Selfishness

"Let nothing be done through selfish ambition or conceit, but in lowliness of mind let each esteem others better than himself" (Phil. 2:3) Miriam's complaint to Moses was pervaded with selfishness. Instead of rejoicing over a plan that would make Israel's life and march more effective, Miriam made it clear that she was miffed over being left out of the inner circle planning. Verse 2 ends with the words, "And the LORD heard it." Let us not think that our peevish complaints about supposed slights are earthbound—heaven is tuned in to our wavelength. God was by no means happy about what He heard from the mouth of Miriam.

6. The Sin of Hate

"But he who hates his brother is in darkness and walks in darkness, and does not know where he is going, because the darkness has blinded his eyes" (1 John 2:11). The sin of Miriam progressed from jealousy to prejudice to hate. If God had not chastened her, there would have been no end to her retrogression. Only the Lord's loving chastening (Heb. 12:6) saved Miriam from permanent spiritual disaster. Sometimes sickness and affliction are our salvation from utter spiritual darkness. True repentance can bring healing of soul and body.

7. The Sin of Foolishness

So Aaron said to Moses, "Oh, my lord! Please do not lay

this sin on us, in which we have <u>done</u> <u>foolishly</u> and in which we have sinned" (Num. 12:11). Miriam's complaint by which she thought she would restore herself to coleadership with Moses (after all, she was the big sister who saved Moses from his ark of bulrushes—Ex. 2:1–10) landed her at the very bottom instead òf at the top. As it turned out, they had to confess their *foolishness,* which had led to leprosy and banishment.

NOTE:

Moses made no defense of himself in answer to the complaint of Aaron and Miriam. The inspired text informs us that Moses was the most humble man on the face of the earth. God Himself defended Moses, His appointed leader (Num. 12:6–8).

The awful leprosy of Miriam was short-lived—she suffered from the affliction and from banishment from the encampment of Israel for seven days as actually and ceremonially unclean. When the leprosy appeared, Aaron at once began to repent and to cry out for forgiveness; we must assume that Miriam joined with Aaron in sincere repentance. Apparently Aaron's part in the rebellion was only the result of Miriam's persuasion, for Aaron did not share in the punishment. Since Aaron was the high priest, leprosy would have defiled the whole priesthood.

When Aaron repented for himself and his sister, Moses cried out to God for the healing of Miriam. The healing resulted, but Miriam had to bear the banishment for seven days. God forgives and heals, but the scars of sin remain; Miriam is not again mentioned in the history of the conquest until her death (Num. 20:1).

What lessons might be drawn from Miriam's story?

Which among the seven sins studied do you find most threatening to you?

In what way might you deal with that?

Miriam's affliction was the result of grievous sins, but God in His infinite mercy answered the prayer of faith of Moses, healing Miriam of her affliction. Many sick people have the impression that their sickness is the result of sin on their part. Many times sickness is simply the result of natural cause and effect. However, if an affliction is a chastening from God, one can be encouraged by the fact that God healed Miriam in answer to believing prayer. Compared with the sins of Miriam, the ordinary person's offenses would be minor. If you are sick and you feel that your sickness is a chastening from God, rejoice in that "whom the LORD loves He chastens." If you have sincerely repented (changed your will and conduct), ask God for healing, or call for the elders; you will in all probability be healed.

How many kinds of modern conduct do you think God might chasten one for in order to effect repentance (change of conduct or purpose)?

Which of Miriam's sins, in your opinion, are common to some church people today?

Using a concordance, how many New Testament scriptures can you find that deal with one or another of Miriam's sins?

Other than in physical affliction, how have you noticed "sickness" manifested in our society?

How might sin be related to these manifestations?

List someone(s) for whom you might pray to be "healed" in these respects.

CASES OF REPENTANCE IN PSALM 107

The psalmist in Psalm 107 paints four word pictures of persons going through a very common human experience; 1) lost wanderers, 2) captives in bondage, 3) the sick and afflicted, 4) sailors lost in a storm. Each of these passes through five phases: self-sufficiency (v. 11), calamity (vv. 12, 16, 18), repentance (v. 19), deliverance (v. 20), and the call to thanksgiving (v. 22). The psalmist's first reference was to Israel's Babylonian captivity and the restoration to their native land. Yet an inspired Bible speaks not only to its original readers, but to people in all ages who share in the same failures, deliverances, and spiritual heights.

The scripture references noted above are taken from several of the word pictures in Psalm 107. The phases are the same in all four descriptions. God not only deals with all transgressors in a broadly similar pattern, but He also saves and rescues by means of a fixed pattern of redemption—namely, conviction of sin, faith, repentance, salvation, and grateful worship.

In Psalm 107, what kind of person and calamity is described in verses 4–9?

What kind of person and calamity is described in verses 10–16?

What kind of person and calamity is described in verses 17–22?

What kind of person and calamity is described in verses 23–32?

    KINGDOM EXTRA

In this psalm, sickness is the punishment for transgression. To transgress is to willfully violate known boundaries of obedience. The punishment, then, is not so much a direct action of God's will as an indirect result of our having violated the blessings within the boundaries of His will, and thus having exposed ourselves to the judgments outside it. However, deliverance may come with genuine repentance. Too often people do not call upon God until calamity strikes. Storms come upon us all, sudden difficulty or severe sickness may arrest us from our unperceived or willful spiritual decline. But the text implies that if the Lord is sought with a contrite heart, crying for deliverance, the calamity may be reversed and result in *both* spiritual and physical healing. The Lord will hear such a cry; and when He does, He heals us with "His word," (v. 20).[2] A beautiful example of this is seen in Jesus' healing of the paralyzed man in Luke 5:17–26.

THE HEALING OF THE PARALYZED MAN
(Luke 5:17–26)

About the earlier life and experience of the paralytic in Luke's story we are told nothing. We can assume that his affliction was in some way related to a past sinful life, because Jesus, when He saw faith demonstrated in a remarkable manner, said to the paralytic, "Your sins are forgiven you."

The awakening and change in the man's heart and mind was no doubt effected by his very dedicated neighbors who, in all likelihood, had witnessed to him about the teachings of Jesus and His great healing power. While the paralyzed man obviously was willing to meet Jesus, he could not by himself journey to where He might be teaching and healing. Actually, he had to overcome a number of obstacles before he would experience deliverance.

First, there was the barrier of resignation to overcome. Many persons handicapped for a long period of time become adjusted to their affliction, resigned to the plight, and even comfortable in it—a psychological barrier. Fortunately the paralytic's benevolent neighbors awakened in him a desire to walk again, to be a part of life.

Second, he must have had a social barrier. His long isolation from active society would have left him timid and retiring and reluctant to be a spectacle to the crowds at a great public event. Again the picture of great deliverance and forgiveness, which his neighbors painted for him of Jesus' compassionate ministry, gave him the courage he needed to make the surrender.

Third, there was a physical barrier—his inability to walk to a meeting sight. This the neighbor friends would overcome for him. Even when multitudes of curious and needy people blocked any access to the door, they scaled an outside ladder to the roof and let him down through an opening made in the tiles, to the very presence of Jesus.

Fourth, a spiritual barrier was placed by Satan. Religious enemies of Jesus were present at the meeting, disputing with Jesus, and denying Jesus' right to forgive sins. Yet once the paralytic had overcome the first obstacles, he, with the help of his unselfish neighbors, made the plunge. In effect, they together had cried out for help to the incarnate God of love and mercy.

Jesus, pausing in His teaching, and sensing the poignant faith-filled appeal of the paralytic and his friends, said, "Man, your sins are forgiven you" (v. 20).

Why do you think Jesus first said, "Your sins are forgiven you," rather than "Take up your bed and go to your house"? Sin is at the bottom of the whole human dilemma. All that a holy God does for us, He does on the basis of a sacrificial offering for sin. Sin must be atoned for in order for Him to have fellowship with us. Sin must be dealt with before healing can come. Jesus could say, "Your sins are forgiven you" because He was on His way to the Cross to be our atoning Sacrifice for sin.

The Pharisees, closing their eyes to Christ's mission as a suffering Savior, denied His right to forgive sin; Jesus answered them with a question, "Which is easier to say, 'Your sins are forgiven you,' or to say, 'Rise up and walk'?" To the casual observer, it would be easier to say, "Your sins are forgiven you," because who could see anything that would deny whether the person was forgiven or not? But to say, "Rise up and walk," one would have to have the power to bring it to pass before the multitude.

However, for Jesus, it was easier to say, "Rise up and walk" because He had the omnipotence to bring the deliverance to pass; but to say, "Your sins are forgiven you," He had to drink the bitter dregs of Calvary's cup; He had to be dedicated to the Cross. "Without shedding of blood there is no remission" of sins (Heb. 9:22). Power is always easier than love and mercy. What good would it have done for Jesus to have said to the paralytic, "Rise up and walk," if He could not also have said, "Your sins are forgiven you"? With healing, the paralyzed man could have lived a few more years in comfort, but with his sins forgiven, he would live forever; he would share in the resurrection of Jesus and be seated with Christ in heavenly places (Eph. 2:1–10).

1. *Spirit-Filled Life Bible* (Nashville, TN: Thomas Nelson Publishers, 1991), 1407, "Word Wealth: 3:2 repent."
2. Ibid., 848, "Kingdom Dynamics: Deliverance from Our 'Destructions.'"

Lesson 4/Healing and the Prayer of Faith

In the biography of Hudson Taylor there is a revealing passage. In a letter written to a friend, dated November 18, 1870, Taylor tells this story. He had been reading in the New Testament in the original Greek. He was reading the Gospel according to St. Mark when, suddenly and strangely, his attention was arrested by a short sentence of three brief words. He turned to his King James edition of the English New Testament and read the familiar words, "Have faith in God," but in the Greek original there was a thought, an insight, which the Authorized Version had failed to render. For this is how Taylor read it: "Hold to the faithfulness of God." The discovery, he said, lit up many dark places of his own thinking. It gave him a big lift. And so it should, for such is the basis of true faith.

God gave to the great missionary, in a time of severe testing, a wise admonition from Mark 11:22. Most of the Bibles render the passage, "Have faith in God," an admonition all believers obey; it is the basis of our Christian experience. But sometimes we forget about the *faithfulness* of God in never forsaking His children in any circumstance of life. In the final analysis, faith is *holding on* to the faithful promises of God, one of which is to heal the body.

One of the finest examples we have in the New Testament of bold faith is the account of the woman who touched the hem of Jesus' garment in spite of her condition, her experience in failure to get help, and the throngs of people who milled between her and Jesus. Stop now, and read about her in Mark 5:21–34. See also Luke 8:43–48. As you read these passages especially watch for the word *touch*.

The key word in this story is touch. Five times in the passage mention is made of the *touch* the woman made to the garment of Jesus. Let us key in on the nature of the woman's touch. It will reveal to us much about the woman and even more about the love, mercy, and wisdom of Jesus. Look at these three characteristics of the woman's vital touch.

IT WAS A TOUCH OF DESPERATION

The woman (we do not know her name) came to Jesus after twelve years of serious illness, which physicians had been unable to cure. Since she had resorted to every avenue of healing known to her, the visit to Jesus was a last desperate hope for help. Not only was she still ill, but she was penniless.

The extremity of her desperation is seen even more clearly when we are aware of her violation of the Law of Moses (Lev. 15). Because of the nature of her illness, she was ceremonially unclean. To mingle with people was for her a violation of the Law for which she could have been stoned. Her elbowing her way through a vast and dense crowd of people was a serious infringement of that Law. She had hoped to get a passing touch of Jesus' garment without being noticed; therefore, she was terrified when Jesus called her out of the crowd.

The vast crowds that followed Jesus made it almost impossible for weak persons to get near Him; and since Jesus was moving as swiftly as possible to fulfill a mission of mercy, with the disciples working to clear a path for Jesus, a slow mover would have found it almost impossible to keep up. That the woman was able to penetrate the swift-moving parade speaks worlds of her desperate determination to reach her goal.

The nature of Jesus' mission was such as to discourage any interruption. He had been summoned by the ruler of the synagogue to come and pray for his daughter who was at the point of death. No one who knew of the urgency of the mission would have attempted normally to cause a delay in the life-and-death mission of the Lord. It would be almost impossible to imagine a scheme more destined for failure than that of the woman; it was a "mission impossible" that had a glorious fulfillment.

IT WAS A TOUCH OF FAITH

With all the obstacles in the way, only a genuinely vital faith would have kept the seeker on her course. She had resolved, "If only I may touch His clothes, I shall be made well."

What do you think might possibly have implanted such resolve in the woman's heart and mind?

It seems very likely that she had some knowledge of the healing power of Jesus. Either she had witnessed a miracle of healing, or some neighbor, friend, or relative had conveyed to her the good news about the mercies of the teacher from Galilee. She appeared to have a deep conviction that to touch Jesus would bring the coveted healing that she had so vainly sought for twelve years. It is quite possible that the Lord imparted that faith to her hungry soul. After all, faith is a gift from the Lord. She did not say, "I hope that this magic touch will give some help"; she said, "If only I may touch His clothes, I shall be made well"! Such a statement has faith written all over it. When Jesus interviewed her, He said to her, "Your faith has made you well."

WORD WEALTH

Faith, *pistis.* Conviction, confidence, trust, belief, reliance, trustworthiness, and persuasion. In the New Testament setting, *pistis* is the divinely implanted principle of inward confidence, assurance, trust and reliance in God and all that He says. The word sometimes denotes the object or content of belief (Acts 6:7).[1]

Believe, *pisteuo.* The verb form of *pistis,* "faith." It means to trust in, have faith in, be fully convinced of, acknowledge, rely on. *Pisteuo* is more than credence in church doctrines or articles of faith. It expresses reliance upon and a personal trust that produces obedience. It includes submission and a positive confession of the lordship of Jesus.[2]

Write a short statement about the importance of, the need for, or the result of *faith* in the following scripture passages.

Matt. 15:28

Matt. 21:22

Mark 16:17

Luke 5:20

Luke 7:9

Luke 7:50

Luke 8:50

Luke 17:5

Acts 6:5, 6

1 Cor. 12:9

THE TOUCH OF BECOMING

It is inspiring to consider here the devotional concept of divine healing's power to restore personhood. It could be said about the woman who touched the hem of Jesus' garment that, considering her poverty, her terminal affliction, and her ceremonial uncleanness which isolated her from society, she was, at least in the eyes of the teeming multitude, a *nobody*. But her touch of desperate faith made her a *somebody*. At her touch, Jesus declared, "<u>Somebody</u> touched me!" The surprised disciples said to Him, "Master, the multitudes throng and press You, and You say, 'Who touched Me?'" But Jesus said, "<u>Somebody</u> touched Me, for I perceived power going out from Me." After reading this passage in Luke 8:43–48, we should forever know that there is a vast difference between "thronging" Jesus and "touching" Him. In a sense all people who attend Gospel meetings are thronging Jesus, but only a small number actually touch Him through positive faith.

It might appear that the "somebody" designation is only a play on words, but reading on we observe that Jesus, in addition, said to the woman, "Daughter, be of good cheer, your faith has made you well." That day a nobody, by human appraisal, became not only a "somebody," she became a "daughter of God." In effect, for a little while she was "everybody"; she was the very center of attention of Jesus, of His disciples, of the vast throng, and even of the messengers from the house of Jairus. All activity ceased until the full meaning of what had happened to her was made clear.

The quest of the modern man is to make a name for himself, to become somebody. But too many are traveling the wrong road. The real road to eternal identity is reached by the confession of Jesus Christ as Savior and Lord. Those who travel His pathway of love will receive a new name that will never be blemished.

The woman probably hoped to touch Jesus without being detected. But when Jesus demanded to know who had touched Him, she could not escape; she then told him the whole account of her desperate maneuver: "She came trembling; and falling down before Him, she declared to Him in the presence of all the people the reason she had touched Him and how she was healed immediately" (v. 47).

Now those who touch Jesus with the touch of faith become a part of His family; they cannot experience His healing virtue without receiving the embrace of His love. The Lord would not let her go away uninformed about what had really happened. She must be told that her faith obtained for her not just a magic cure, but an eternal relationship. She received, not just something: she received Christ—the most important Person in the whole universe. He tells her that what she experienced was not merely the end of bodily suffering, but also the beginning of a new vital and eternal blessedness.

It is possible that the news of the woman who touched the hem of Jesus' garment became widespread, for we read the following about similar healings on a larger scale, "Wherever He entered, into villages, cities, or in the country, they laid the sick in the marketplaces, and begged Him that they might <u>just touch the hem of His garment</u>. And as many as touched Him were made well" (Mark 6:56).

It must be observed that while all this was happening for the desperate woman, the ruler of the synagogue, who had summoned Jesus to pray for his dying daughter, anxiously, and seemingly futilely, waited for Jesus to come. While he waited, apparently in vain, his daughter expired. Why would Jesus let a "nobody" detain Him while the daughter of the ruler of the synagogue was dying. Why would Jesus permit Himself to arrive "too late"?

Read Luke 8:49–56. At what point do you see faith's action pivot toward power?

Where might faith have surrendered to doubt?

Jesus never arrives nor acts "too late." Jesus knew well what was happening at the house of Jairus, as Luke recounts in the joyous end of the story.

Jairus's experience reminds us of the death and resurrection of Lazarus (John 11). Martha said to Jesus, "Lord, if You had been here, my brother would not have died." Jesus answered her, "Your brother will rise again. . . . I am the resurrection and the life." Jesus is never in a hurry; He never arrives too late. Nothing is hidden from His eyes. He never forgets our needs. He never fails. He could say to the family of Jairus, "Do not be afraid; only <u>believe</u>."

A very important lesson can be learned from Jesus' delay with the afflicted woman. God never lacks time to finish His works of mercy. Many people's faith has been weakened by the thought that God has so many prayers to answer that He could never hear individual requests. Satan tempts us to ask ourselves, "How can I expect God to answer my prayer when there are millions of needy people, all around the world, who are bombarding the throne of grace with petitions, many of which are more important than mine?" "How can Jesus walk by my side when billions of people are expecting the same nearness?" These are troubling doubts, but we can find assurance in the Bible, remembering that our God is both omnipresent and omnipotent and has given His Holy Spirit to abide *personally* in each one of us! He is an infinite God who has no limitations of space, time, or circumstances. It might help to remind ourselves that even feeble man has been able to get everyone's name on a central computer bank, and that with man-made television, we can witness many things that go on in the world. If by human means the bank balance of anyone anywhere can be verified, the Maker of the measureless universe can certainly keep current with anything that is happening in it.

FAITH ALIVE

A passage from the prophet Isaiah reminds us of the unlimited power and wisdom of our God;

"To whom then will you liken Me,
Or *to whom* shall I be equal?" says the Holy One.
Lift up your eyes on high,
And see who has created these *things*,
Who brings out their host by number;
He calls them all by name,
By the greatness of His might
And the strength of *His* power;
Not one is missing.
Why do you say, O Jacob,
And speak, O Israel:
"My way is hidden from the LORD,
And my just claim is passed over by my God"?
Have you not known?
Have you not heard?
The everlasting God, the LORD,
The Creator of the ends of the earth,
Neither faints nor is weary.
His understanding is unsearchable. (Is. 40:25–28)

Take time tonight. Look at the star-strewn sky. Think then on this passage. Rejoice in God's *power* and in His personal care for you!

The woman who touched Jesus' garment is an example of one to whom God gave a gift of quality faith. Another excellent example of surprisingly great faith is the centurion (a Roman soldier with authority over one hundred men), whose servant Jesus healed. The account is related in Luke 7:1–10. Open your Bible and read this passage, taking special note of the centurion's reasoning with Jesus.

The centurion was a very remarkable person. Jesus marveled at him, as if He were surprised to find a Gentile with unexcelled faith. The centurion might be called "the man who surprised the Lord." Contrary to expectation, Roman centurions in the New Testament are found to be men of admirable character. There are several very surprising qualities in this centurion of Capernaum:

1. He was surprisingly human. He loved his servant (slave). Many Roman military men would have left a sick slave to die. This centurion exerted influence upon the elders of the

Jews, for whom he had built a synagogue, to persuade Jesus to heal his servant. Such compassion from a Roman military man marked him as a man of unusual goodness and depth of character.

2. The Roman captain in charge of keeping order in Capernaum was also a surprisingly generous man. He had built, at his own expense, a synagogue for the Jews. His position did not require of him such unselfishness. The Jewish elders even stated that he loved their nation. Many educated Romans no longer took seriously the gods and goddesses of paganism; some of them had adopted the Jewish faith. Our centurion, while not likely a proselyte to Judaism, was certainly respectful of it, and at the same time a sincere believer in Jesus.

3. The centurion was a surprisingly humble man. The elders said of him that he was "deserving," or "worthy" of this favor. The centurion in his message to Jesus said, "I am not worthy that You should enter under my roof." This he said in spite of being one of the most prominent citizens of Capernaum.

4. He had surprising perception. He understood the secret of true authority. As a military officer, he had absolute authority over his soldiers. It is said of Roman military discipline that soldiers could be marched over a cliff if the officer did not cry, "Halt!" Yet wise officers did not overstep their authority. This centurion understood authority because he was himself under the authority of his superior. It is doubtful that anyone could understand authority without serving under it. The centurion could expect perfect obedience from his soldiers; he was prepared to give the same respect to those over him. The centurion was ready to give to Jesus full obedience, at the same time he knew that all forces were under the authority of Jesus, as Jesus was under the authority of the Father. He perceived that Jesus had the authority and power to speak his slave well from a distance. Perhaps he had read the psalm that says, "He sent His word and healed them" (Ps. 107:20). The centurion's word over his soldiers was final; Jesus' word over all the forces of nature and over every kind of circumstance was final. This the centurion perceived.

5. Jesus said about the centurion, "I have not found such great faith, not even in Israel." Just as the woman knew that if she could *touch the robe* of Jesus she would be made whole, the centurion knew beyond all doubt that, if Jesus *spoke the word* of healing, his slave would be made whole; and so it was. Both of these had quality faith, but the woman needed a physical touch to release her faith—the centurion needed only the word of Jesus for the healing of his distant servant. When he left Jesus to return home, he knew that he would find a well servant when he arrived.

Do not, however, devalue the physical contact, the laying on of hands of the elders or of another person; many who pray regularly for the sick point to the value of a point of contact. Some people can pray alone with effective faith; others are helped by the prayer and presence of another person. Noticeable effectiveness in prayer results from group intercession. In a great Holy Ghost revival in a large city, many attributed their miraculous healings to daily morning meetings where the truth about healing was taught from the Bible, and healing testimonies were exchanged. When hands were laid on them in the public meetings, a very high percentage of the sick were healed. "Faith *comes* by hearing, and hearing by the word of God" (Rom. 10:17).

 ## Faith Alive

In this chapter we have been studying *healing* and *faith*. Attention has been given to two New Testament passages about persons who manifested strong faith in the healing power and ministry of the Lord. In these accounts many hints can be found that will enable us today to appropriate the bodily healing which Jesus' atoning work has made available to us. On the surface the two accounts have very little in common. In both cases the faith manifested appeared to be given by the Lord. Both principals were persons from whom we would normally expect little faith, yet both manifested outstanding faith—faith that God bestowed. The centurion manifested a maturity of faith that surprised even the Lord.

If these persons—one an afflicted woman who practically lived in isolation, the other a military man who spent most of his time in an army barracks—could possess such extraordinary faith, there is no reason why any of us cannot, through the study of the Word and a daily set time of prayer, possess a quality faith. We can be fully capable of laying hold upon the faithful promises of God. God's promises encompass every possible need of man for body or soul. God does not condemn us for resorting to any proper remedies for our ills, since He is the maker of all the remedies that wise men discover. But there is a blessing and anointing imparted by divine healing that no other means supplies. We can surround any procedure with prayer with happy results; still, nothing quite draws us as close to Jesus as to hear Him whisper to our innermost being, "Your faith has made you well."

1. *Spirit-Filled Life Bible* (Nashville, TN: Thomas Nelson Publishers, 1991), 1492, "Word Wealth: 11:22 faith."
2. Ibid., 1704, "Word Wealth: 10:9 believe."

Lesson 5/Healing and Obedience

The purpose of this chapter is to point out the relationship and importance of obedience to divine healing as well as to all the Lord's blessings.

The author of Hebrews wrote the following about the example Jesus Himself set for us in obedience to the Father: "Though He was a Son, *yet* He learned obedience by the things which He suffered. And having been perfected, He became the author of eternal salvation to all who obey Him" (Heb. 5:8). This quotation makes reference to the critical resolve of Jesus in the Garden of Gethsemane, "If it is possible, let this cup pass from Me, nevertheless, not as I will, but as You *will*" (Matt. 26:39). If implicit obedience to the Father's will was essential to Christ's work of our redemption, how much more important is obedience to the Lord by those who seek His blessings!

We will first examine 2 Kings 5:1–15 and its emphasis on obedience. Open your Bible to this passage, and note the following as you read:

Who are the central characters?

What is the central message?

Where is faith's pivot point of action?

Here is a story about a great general of the armies of Syria, but he was a leper. He was highly successful as a military leader, but he was a leper. He was strong and highly esteemed by the king of Syria, but he was a leper. The greatest wish of the king and of Naaman the leper was to be rid of the dreaded and fatal disease, a futile hope. Leprosy, a "type" of sin in the Old Testament, was thought to be incurable; being free from the degrading curse was, for all intents and purposes, his "impossible dream."

Yet God in His providential plan to reveal His power and majesty to the Syrian king and his court had placed a humble and faithful maid in the household of Naaman. The captive Israelite girl was certain that if Naaman could visit the great Prophet Elisha, of her country, he would be cured of his leprosy. Three things about the maid stand out: 1) she was a devout believer in the Lord God, 2) she sensed her providential placement in the home of the afflicted general; and 3) she had the spiritual courage to give witness to God's saving and healing power.

Read the following paragraph; then list three lessons the servant girl illustrates.

All of us who want to be used by God need to maintain our dedication and faith in God's redeeming power. This we do through prayer, Bible study, and frequent witness. Furthermore, it is important at all costs to avoid Satan's trap that would entangle us in a bondage to daily routines. We must maintain our conviction that we are the Lord's servants who are where we are for the purpose of being a witness to His power and mercy. Finally, we must pray regularly that God will give us the victory over fear and impart to us the gift of boldness to let our light shine in dark places. Had it not been for the faithful witnessing captive girl, Naaman would have died of leprosy, and Syria would have been devoid of a great leader who believed in and highly exalted the Lord God. The Jewish girl might have withdrawn in resentment of her captivity, but she obeyed God and her faithfulness was told in a book that would be read for thousands of years. God has another book in heaven that is being written about His obedient children. "Therefore we also, since we are surrounded by so great a cloud of witnesses, let us lay aside every weight, and the sin which so easily ensnares *us*, and let us run with endurance the race that is set before us" (Heb. 12:1).

The servant girl illustrates these principles of faithful witness:

1.

2.

3.

Many times God passes over the people in high places, using rather the humble to accomplish His purposes. Naaman made his approach to Elisha through the avenues of the king of Syria and then of the king of Israel, but the approach ended in a cul-de-sac—the utter consternation of Israel's king. Fortunately for Naaman, God revealed to Elisha the leper's coming, with the result that Naaman ended up at Elisha's front door in expectation that the prophet would march forth ceremoniously, waving his hand, and pronounce him healed. Was he disappointed! Elisha did not appear; he instead sent a messenger ordering him to go wash seven times in the muddy Jordan.

Naaman was furious, so angry that he almost went home empty. His wise attendants persuaded him to be obedient to the prophet's commanded prerequisite to healing. His initial unwillingness to obey almost prevented his miracle. Let us look at the reasons for Naaman's reluctance to obey; perhaps we will see a parallel to some of our own temptations to disobey what we think are unreasonable demands:

1. First of all, Naaman thought that dipping in the muddy Jordan River was beneath his dignity; after all, he was a four-star general. His was a reluctance of pride instead.

Have you ever rebelled at going forward, or kneeling down, or letting someone put oil on your head, or worse—spending a week in prayer and fasting?

Have you ever shrunk from admitting that you are sick or that you have symptoms of a needy condition?

2. Naaman also objected to the impersonal procedure. He expected a ceremony instead of simple obedience. He was looking forward to having a famous prophet give him a more elaborate ceremony. He wanted spectacular magic commensurate with his elaborate military maneuvers. Many people who travel miles to be prayed for by a big-name evangelist never go to the altar in their home church. Although many are healed in large crusades, sometimes the Lord wants to teach us that He is everywhere present and that He answers believing prayer without "respect of persons or places." The healing covenant in the Book of James leads us to believe that the primary place of preference for healing is the local church.

Examine various healings recorded in the Bible that show the importance of obedience in the deliverance.

- Miriam had to remain outside the camp for seven days before her healing of leprosy became effective.
- When bitten by fiery serpents as a punishment for their constant murmuring, the children of Israel were required to look away to a bronze serpent on a pole in order to receive healing from their mortal bites.
- King Hezekiah, when he was given a death sentence, was commanded to place on his boil a poultice of figs.

Some have suggested that the poultice was a medicinal remedy often prescribed in antiquity. However, it is clear that the figs did not cure Hezekiah; it was the divine power and mercy that extended the king's life for another fifteen years. The application of the poultice of figs was an act of *obedience*.

WORD WEALTH

Obedience, *hupakoe.* From *hupo,* "under," and *akouo,* "to hear" or "to listen." The word signifies attentive hearing, to listen with compliant submission, assent, and agreement. It is used for obedience in general, for obedience to God's commands, and for Christ's obedience.[1]

Why, in your opinion, did the Lord require of Naaman to dip seven times in the river Jordan?

Why did Miriam have to be isolated for seven days as an act of obedience?

Why do you think the children of Israel were required to make and look to bronze serpents in order to be delivered from the fatal bites?

Give a brief explanation of the poultice of figs that King Hezekiah was commanded to apply to his fatal boil. Was it medicine or an act of obedience?

Who is our finest example of obedience to the Father?

The requirement of some act of obedience as a requisite to healing is not something exacted in the Old Testament only. The New Testament gives significant examples.

Read Luke 17:11–19. What act of obedience is directed? What are the results?

THOUGHT-PROVOKER REGARDING HEALING

There are believers who, in their life-style, violate laws of proper diet and exercise, or who abuse their bodies by overwork and exertion, or who are addicted to harmful substances. When illness results from such abuses, it is not likely that the Lord would continue healing that person; any doctor or surgeon would advise the patient to desist from the harmful practice. Our bodies are temples of the Holy Spirit, which we should respect. If we ask God to heal a sickness caused by abuse, is it unreasonable that He should make a change in life-style a condition for the healing?

Another New Testament example of healing through obedience is that of the blind man in John 9:1–12. Read this passage and note the following:

1. What common but faulty presupposition is stated by the disciples?

2. What act of obedience does Jesus direct?

3. How did what happened glorify God as Jesus said? (v. 3)

Notice from this story:

First, the man's blindness from birth obviously was not the result of, or a punishment for, sin. Nor was the affliction a result of some sin on the part of his parents. The disciples of

Jesus conjectured about whether the blindness was caused by the man's sin or that of his parents. Jesus explained to them that the malady existed so that its healing by the Son of God would bring glory to God.

Second, those who resist miracles and divine healings, saying they were given only in Jesus' day to demonstrate Jesus' deity, cannot find support in this case. Jesus explained that the miracle of healing of the blind man was providentially planned to demonstrate the works of God. The works of God need demonstration in *all* ages, and today as much as ever. The deity of Jesus has been demonstrated for all time by His Resurrection. But now, the works of God need to be brought to light in all ages that men may praise and worship God.

Third, no medicinal value can be attributed to the clay or the saliva of Jesus, because the healing did not happen until the clay pack was washed away in the pool of Siloam. What healed the blind man? the clay? the saliva? the water? None of these. The act of obedience was the condition for the healing, the actual healing was the work of the Holy Spirit at the word of Jesus.

Yet another New Testament example of healing on the condition of a simple act of obedience is found in Mark 3:1–5:

> And He entered the synagogue again, and a man was there who had a withered hand. So they watched Him closely, whether He would heal him on the Sabbath, so that they might accuse Him. And He said to the man who had the withered hand, "Step forward." Then He said to them, "Is it lawful on the Sabbath to do good or to do evil, to save life or to kill?" But they kept silent. And when He had looked around at them with anger, being grieved by the hardness of their hearts, He said to the man, "Stretch out your hand." And he stretched *it* out, and his hand was restored as whole as the other.

This act of obedience described by Mark was much less involved than those in the cases of the lepers and the man born blind. A man with a withered hand is commanded to step forward and to stretch forth his hand. This act was, however, a little more difficult circumstantially than some of the others. Jesus was being followed and criticized by the scribes and Pharisees; here in their own synagogue they were just waiting to see if Jesus would heal someone on the Sabbath day so that they might accuse him of violating the Law of Moses. The rabbis had concluded that the healing art might be practiced on the Sabbath if it were a matter of life and death, but the healing of a withered arm would not qualify. Jesus might have waited until the next day to heal the arm, but He desired to teach that the Sabbath was made for man, and not man for the Sabbath.

Jesus knew that the leaders of the synagogue would oppose healing on the Sabbath, but He also knew, being the Creator of all things and of all laws, and being the Lord of the Sabbath (Mark 2:28), that to heal the man would not only make him a whole person, but also keep him from being a roadside beggar. With a divine touch the man would be blessed spiritually, physically, economically, and socially. Jesus turned to the man and commanded, "Step forward." Will the man obey Jesus contrary to the teaching of his synagogue? The decision was not easy, but he obeyed Jesus and became a whole person. Even the simplest acts of obedience are not always easy.

Jesus often said to the sick, "Take up your bed and walk." Obedience required at least an effort. Those who made the effort found that they were healed. The simplest act of obedience is seen in the story in John 5:2–9. Read of the man who had been sick for thirty-eight years.

Why do you think Jesus said, "Do you want to be made well?"

Do you think there are sick today who do not truly want healing? If so, why?

BEHIND THE SCENES

"The last phrase of John 5:3, 4 is omitted in some ancient Greek manuscripts of John. The statements may reflect a popular tradition associated with the pool that the bubbling of the waters (v. 7), which some scholars feel was caused by an intermittent spring, was supernaturally caused by an angel. Irrespective of the source of the waters being stirred, the testimony of God's healing grace was nonetheless present."[2]

We have studied stories of difficult, simple, and complex acts of obedience as related to receiving divine healing. We have seen that obedience is essential to our relationship with the Lord. It could be possible that God who sees all things from the beginning and who knows perfectly what is the very best for our lives, might require of us to put our whole lives on the altar of service.

Give three scriptural examples in the New Testament of healings that called for some act of obedience.

Why do you think that obedience is important to the whole Christian life?

How large a demand do you think God would ever make on one's life?

FAITH ALIVE

God may not demand a dramatic response to every healing act, such as offering oneself for mission work in some distant field. However, our surrender to the lordship of Jesus does require that we surrender to His will and seek to discover and know His will for our lives. He has some form of service for every true believer. The Christian life is not a spectator sport. The stadium of the heavens is filled with those who have already run their race on earth. We on earth have been given the baton to run our part of the race. God has not called anyone to just watch the race. We are called to stand on the promises, not merely to "sit on the premises." Sometimes it may take an illness or an affliction to awaken us to our need to make a deeper dedication, a fuller obedience.

There are some kinds of afflictions for some people which seem to respond only to medical or surgical treatment. Resorting to medicine or surgery, however, does not eliminate the divine healing factor from one's recovery. Prayer, together with other therapy, can still be a spiritual blessing. Before anything can work successfully, we may have to say a big "yes" to God.

Throughout the Christian pilgrimage of life the key word is *obedience.*

> "If you love Me, keep My commandments. . . . He who has My commandments and keeps them, it is he who loves Me. And he who loves Me will be loved by My Father, and I will love him and manifest Myself to him." . . . Jesus answered and said to him, "If anyone loves Me, he will keep My word; and My Father will love him, and We will come to him and make Our home with him." (John 14:15, 21, 23)

1. *Spirit-Filled Life Bible* (Nashville, TN: Thomas Nelson Publishers, 1991), 1763, "Word Wealth: 10:5 obedience."
2. Ibid., 1581, note on 5:4.

Lesson 6/Divine Healing and the Cross

There are no likenesses on earth of the marvel of Christ's atonement for us—of the full work that Jesus accomplished for us when He died upon the Cross. From before the foundation of the world He purposed to provide a complete covering for whosoever would believe (1 Pet. 2:24). Foreseeing that man would fall and that his fall would bring upon him a curse of misery, affliction, and death, Christ willed to take upon Himself that curse and to set believing mankind free. This action of His "complete covering" of our sins *and* providing all the benefits of our salvation is often called "the atonement." It notes the lessons and Old Testament pictures of the Savior who would come (Lev. 17:11).

 **WORD WEALTH**

Make atonement, *chaphar.* To cover, make atonement, make reconciliation, to pacify or appease; to clear, purge or cleanse. This verb occurs 100 times. The primary meaning of *chaphar* may be "to cover." An important derivative is the word *kippur* (atonement), a familiar term due to its use in *Yom Kippur,* the Day of Atonement; see Lev. 23:27, 28; Num. 15:25. "Appease" and "make reconciliation" translate *chaphar* in Gen. 32:20 and Dan. 9:24 respectively.[1]

There is a marvelous *breadth* of provision for us in Christ's Cross. "Here [in 1 Peter 2:22–25] He is our Redeemer; Christ's vicarious death makes possible our response of death **to sins** (repentance) and life for God (**righteousness**). This is New Testament Christian conversion in its broadest application, which Peter describes when he says, **"by whose stripes you were healed."** Peter's intent in quoting Isaiah 53:5 is to show that personal wholeness—mental, psychological, physical, and spiritual—flows from this conversion."[2]

Christ's atoning death released for believing mankind a healing stream for the whole person—spiritual healing and physical healing. The first Adam plunged humanity into an affliction of body, mind, and spirit; the last Adam rescued fallen humanity with a healing of body, mind, and spirit. The fall was total; the rescue, too, was total. But believers are a new creation in Christ Jesus (2 Cor. 5:17) in which "creation" *all things* hold the prospect of becoming new!

The complete "atonement"—covering—that Jesus provided on the Cross obtained for mankind so many blessings and benefits. Write a personal response to your own reading of each one here, noticing the distinct blessing each emphasizes, and how each blessing has applied or can apply to your life right now.

1. The blessing that Jesus became the *Savior* of mankind (Matt. 1:21).

2. The blessing that all who believe are *justified* (Acts 13:39; Rom. 5:1).

3. The blessing that we can receive *cleansing* by the blood of Christ (1 John 1:7).

4. The blessing of *sanctification* for our lives and living (Heb. 13:12).

5. The blessing of divine healing is made available (1 Pet. 2:24).

6. The provision of unlimited or universal blessings is opened to us (John 14:13; Eph. 1:3).

In the beginning, as soon as man fell, God gave a promise of atonement. In Genesis, chapter three, which recounts man's fall, we have divine assurance that Satan, the cause and perpetuator of the curse would be defeated by the "seed of woman" (a term for the Incarnate Son of God). "And I will put enmity between you and the woman, and between your seed and her Seed; He shall bruise your head, and you shall bruise His heel" (Gen. 3:15). The bruising of Jesus' heel was His death on the Cross by which He would accomplish our redemption from the curse and the effective defeat of Satan whose works issue in our sin and sickness. John wrote that Jesus came to destroy the works of the Devil: "He who sins is of the devil, for the devil has sinned from the beginning. For this purpose the Son of God was manifested, that He might destroy the works of the devil" (1 John 3:8).

The Old Testament closes with a prophecy that Jesus would bring healing: "But to you who fear My name the Sun of Righteousness shall arise with healing in His wings (Mal. 4:2). He whom John called the "light of the world" came into the darkness of the world; His healing rays are mankind's blessed cure for the guilt of sin and the oppression of sickness.

In the center of the Old Testament the Lord has placed the most complete description of the atoning work of Him who would be bruised for our iniquities and lashed for our healing. Read all of Isaiah 53:3–12 first, then think through the following reference from the *Spirit-Filled Life Bible*.

KINGDOM EXTRA

Isaiah 53 clearly teaches that bodily healing is included in the atoning work of Christ, His suffering, and His Cross. The Hebrew words for "griefs" and "sorrows" (v. 4) specifically mean physical affliction. This is verified in the fact that Matthew 8:17 says that this Isaiah text is being exemplarily fulfilled in Jesus' healing people of human sickness and other physical need.

Further, that the words "borne" and "carried" refer to Jesus' atoning work on the Cross is made clear by the fact that they are the same words used to describe Christ's bearing our sins (see v. 11; also 1 Pet. 2:24). These texts unequivocally link the grounds of provision for both our salvation and our healing to the atoning work of Calvary. Neither is automatically appropriated, however; for each provision—a soul's eternal salvation or a person's temporal, physical healing—must be received by faith. Christ's work on the Cross makes each possible; simple faith receives each as we choose. Incidentally, a few contend that Isaiah's prophecy about sickness was fulfilled completely by the one-day healings described by Matthew 8:17. A close look, however, will show that the word "fulfilled" often applies to an action that extends throughout the whole church age. (See Is. 42:1–4; Matt. 12:14–17.)[3]

IS HEALING FOR TODAY?

How can we be certain that, on the basis of Christ's death on the Cross, God's healing graces are available to us today?

1. We can be certain that bodily healing is included in the atoning work of Christ because the Word of God says that it is. Isaiah states in 53:4 that He bore *(nasa)* our griefs, and carried *(sabal)* our sorrows. In verses 11 and 12 Isaiah applies exactly the same words—*bore* and *carried*—to our "iniquity" and "sin." In other words, the action of saving and healing are inseparably linked. Jesus, quoting from Isaiah in Matthew 8:17, translates the Hebrew words for "griefs" and "sorrows" to mean "infirmities" and "sicknesses." Thus, Isaiah says that Jesus bore and carried *both*—our infirmities and sicknesses, as well as our sins and iniquities. Therefore if Jesus' work on the

Cross covered our sins and iniquities, it is also there that He covered our infirmities and diseases.

Matthew 8:16, 17 makes clear that Jesus dealt with both spiritual and *physical* sicknesses and diseases: "When evening had come, they brought to Him many who were demon-possessed. And He cast out the spirits with a word, and healed all who were sick, that it might be fulfilled which was spoken by Isaiah the prophet, saying: 'He Himself took our infirmities and bore *our* sicknesses.'"

From this we conclude that if the sick people of Jesus' day were healed on the basis of Isaiah's prophecy about Christ's atoning sacrifice *even before it was completed,* then we may be confident of healings being provided for us today.

2. Christians of any century can be assured of healing in the Atonement because Christ's atonement was an infinite redemption. Since Jesus Christ is infinite—eternal—whatever He does as our Savior and Substitute will apply to all needs for all time, until He returns. Read each of the following references and write your own comments on what is said about the Lord's unchanging ways and promises:

Mal. 3:6

Heb. 13:8

James 1:17

3. We can expect Christ to heal today because healing the sick is one of the certain signs He promised would follow those who believed (Mark 16:17, 18). Jesus said one power-sign that would confirm the preaching of the gospel to all the world was that when believers would lay hands on the sick, they would recover. Just as we are commissioned to preach to all nations the saving death of "Christ crucified," we have the privilege to declare the promise of healing for the sick who have faith to believe.

The same gospel that offers the power of God to save from sin also offers healing power to heal sickness. In the Book of Acts the apostles went out preaching the same gospel of the kingdom which Jesus commanded them, with the same signs following. Since the same signs followed in the post-apostolic church, was there ever a cutoff line? No! Jesus hasn't changed! There has never been a time in church history when God's healing power ceased, except when the spiritual level of the church has been low. But whenever revival has returned, the full New Testament power and blessing has been available and manifest. This is not to say that the degree or number of healing manifestations in their midst is a measure of spirituality for all Christians, for some simply have not received teaching. But where this truth is taught and received, God heals people, as we implicitly believe and trust His promises.

4. Believers can be certain that the Lord still heals today because the same Holy Spirit that the Father sent upon the church in answer to the prayer of the Son will continue to abide in the church until Christ's coming again. In view of the Spirit's coming to abide, Jesus promised that "greater works" than those which He did would be done by the church. Some ask whether the "greater" means greater in dimensions, in quality, or greater in quantity. There is no way we can know, but we are certainly not called to limit what Jesus said. The same Holy Spirit through whom Jesus worked miracles is continuing to take the things of Christ and show them unto us, and that includes His wonderful works of healing and deliverance.

That Jesus did work His healing ministry through the power of the Holy Spirit is seen in His announcement to the synagogue in Nazareth (Luke 4:18, 19). Jesus was quoting from the prophet Isaiah (Is. 61:1), who predicted that the Servant of Yahweh would come in "the fullness of time" to present, in the power of the Spirit of God, glad tidings of salvation, healing of the body, and hope for the downtrodden and the captives of Satan. A major theme of Isaiah was that of "The Anointed Servant of Yahweh." He is introduced in Isaiah 11:1, 2 and appears again in Isaiah 42:1, where the full scope of His saving and healing mission is described. The central portrait of the Anointed Servant of Yahweh is found in Isaiah 53, where it is made crystal clear that He would not only come in power to establish a kingdom, but He would do it by way of the Cross, upon which He would offer the infinite sacrifice, purchase salvation and healing for all believers, cancel Satan's curse, and destroy his kingdom of darkness. The Holy Spirit's anointing was promised to carry out these promises—to fulfillment.

Jesus later promised to send the same Holy Spirit to anoint the church (Acts 2:1–4), that by His same "anointing of the Spirit," multitudes would be saved and multitudes healed of all kinds of bodily afflictions. Read each of the following passages and note how He did this, and what evidence this gives that He will do the same today: Acts 5:14–16; 14:3; 19:11, 12.

Jesus promised to send the Holy Spirit as the "Comforter," "Paraclete," or "Helper." The Greek word means "one who comes alongside to help." He is still "helping" the healing of the sick when prayer is offered in faith—healing miraculously and instantly, healing over a season of time by assisting natural recuperation processes, and also attending with His grace the work of trained medical professionals.

5. Not only can believers receive healing when they are sick; God's Word seems to imply a provision and expectation of sustained health is afforded through Christ's Cross. The passage that seems to clearly evidence this is 3 John 2, 3: "Beloved, I pray that you may prosper in all things and <u>be in health, just as your soul prospers</u>. For I rejoiced greatly when brethren came and testified of the truth *that is* in you, just as you walk in the truth."

It has been stated that salutations were often used to wish for the recipient "health" and "prosperity," and that John's salutation may have been only a polite gesture rather than a divine revelation of God's provision of divine health for all believers. And taking the Bible seriously, we *do* see the linking of "soul" and "body" paralleled in receiving the benefits of the Cross as provisions for abundance of *all* such graces. God does not desire poverty and affliction for His children any more than He desires sin for them. The Lord has promised to supply all our needs according to His riches in glory.

Still, this provision should not be mistaken as an assurance that we will not suffer storms, trials, or tribulations. In fact,

Jesus told His disciples that in this world they would suffer tribulation. Peter cautioned the recipients of his epistle not to think it a strange thing that they would experience fiery trials (1 Pet. 4:12, 13). We are reminded that tribulation works patience, hope, and so on. The believer's unshakable assurance is that God will not permit us to be tried beyond our ability to triumph (1 Cor. 10:13). We can go beyond this and claim that all things will be made to work together for good for those who love the Lord. We can rise even higher and exult over being, in Christ, "more than conquerors" (Rom. 8:28–37).

WORD WEALTH

Health, *hugiaino.* Compare "hygiene" and "hygienic." To be sound in body, in good health. Metaphorically, the word refers to sound doctrine (1 Tim. 1:10; 2 Tim. 4:3; Titus 2:1); sound words (1 Tim. 6:3; 2 Tim. 1:13); and soundness in the faith (Titus 1:13; 2:1).[4]

Hugiaino is the word used in 3 John 2, discussed above. Look up the other references cited here and write a paragraph summarizing the full spectrum of "health" as demonstrated by these texts: physical, mental, spiritual.

PAUL'S THORN

Some scholars point to the apostle Paul's experience as a caution against believing too strongly in divine health as a privilege of believers. They point to Paul's "thorn in the flesh" as a proof of Paul's ill health. There have been a number of theories put forth to identify Paul's thorn, yet nowhere is it described for certain. We know from 2 Corinthians 12:7 only that: 1) it was satanic in its nature ("messenger of Satan"); 2) it was to shield him from pride ("lest I be exalted"); and 3) it also seems to have been physical ("thorn in the *flesh*"). He had requested deliverance from the Lord, who bade him look to the sufficiency of divine grace. Paul was a very special servant whose life was unique. However, no one should claim "Paul's thorn" as an argument against divine, health-sustaining grace.

Grace *did* and does abound amid trial, and Paul's case argues *for* this grace, not against it.

Read 2 Corinthians 12:1–10 and record your thoughts about "Paul's thorn," and the meaning of this passage to you.

To Conclude

Before leaving this thought of promised health and prosperity, it should be pointed out that all God's provisions and promises are conditional. John extended his wish to people who were walking in truth and living in truth, which means that they were living fully in all the light that the Lord had shone into their hearts and minds (vv. 3, 4).

A case of Jesus Himself not only promising salvation, but alluding to the healing within that "great salvation," is in John 3:14–16. "As Moses" references Numbers 21:4–9. Examine these passages together, and see if you think that the saving event to which Jesus referred, is a type of His work of redemption, embracing *both* salvation from sin and healing of sickness and disease. If we today can look back to Christ's atoning work on the Cross as the grounds for our salvation from sin, so also can we look to that same redemption for our sicknesses. And since His saving power from sin has not ceased, neither has His healing power for our bodies.

What verses in Isaiah 53 promise that Christ on the Cross would bear and carry our sins and sicknesses?

Give several scripture passages that promise that the Lord does not change.

What are some of the signs that will follow those who believe?

What power does the church still have that will guarantee the permanence of the healing blessing?

During the history of the church, what conditions in the church appeared to diminish the manifestation of healing power?

What conditions in the life of the church have seemed to bring a reoccurrence of healings?

If our bodies as well as our souls have been bought with the same price of the blood of Jesus, how does that fact assure us of the continuation of the healing blessing?

What balance would you note in your belief about health and prosperity for faithful believers?

   FAITH ALIVE

In the previous chapters we have studied the healing covenants of both the Old and the New Testaments; we have discovered that the Cross of Christ is the very center of divine revelation; having viewed the Cross as the fountain from which the twofold stream of salvation and healing flows, we have learned that faith is the key that opens the floodgates of divine blessing for soul and body. We have also learned about the need for repentance when sin and disobedience have blocked the manifestation of God's healing blessings. It was seen that healing sometimes is delayed until needed obedience has been rendered.

The present lesson has put in focus the atoning work of Christ showing that the atonement has given access to God for both the believing sinners and the afflicted. The central teaching of this chapter clearly demonstrates that, since Christ in His atoning work carried both our transgressions and our diseases, both blessings are given for the entire church age. It should be clear to all who read the Scriptures carefully, that healing and salvation were intended to go together until the Lord returns; healing did not cease at some ill-defined cut-off point in history. Christ, crucified and risen, "*is* the same yesterday, today, and forever" (Heb. 13:8).

To most of the readers of this book these truths are not new, although perhaps they are taken for granted. However, our faith is usually strengthened by giving reemphasis to what we already know doctrinally. Almost everyone has at least some minor physical weakness or undefined symptom of body malfunction. Most of these we overlook or alleviate with popping an over-the-counter pill. Since our bodies are the temples of the Holy Spirit, redeemed by the blood of Christ, we can be certain that the Lord is interested in the health of our bodies.

Every day, in our prayer times, we would do well to pray for health and strength for that day. If we feel symptoms, we have the privilege of praying specifically for relief. Whatever therapeutic treatment we choose, our bodily needs should be taken first to the throne of grace. Every time that we experience a healing touch from the loving Lord, our faith builds and increases. If we take the small things to God, it becomes easier to trust Him with the larger problems. If we go to God only when our needs reach disastrous proportions, we will lack the faith to truly believe.

A word of caution! Prayer for healing should *never* make one an enemy of medicine's provision or medical aid as a resource from God. For example, if we pray about a small symptom that only gets more severe instead of less, we should consult a physician. Resorting to the physician does not eliminate Jesus, the Great Physician. Pray that the physician will discover the problem and find an effective remedy. Even the remedies work better when faith in God's healing power accompanies the medical therapy. Often miraculous recovery will occur when prayer accompanies medical and surgical treatment; nothing is impossible with God. *All* healing is from God. Satan has no desire to see humankind experience *any* blessing. So there is really no other healing than divine healing, and Christians may benefit from medical aid and resource. In fact, many physicians and surgeons admit that they trust God to help them speed recovery.

But go to God first; His healing power is real. He hears and answers prayer. The experience of direct divine healing is one of the most glorious experiences that a believer enjoys. God's healing blessings enhance our witness to others. There is a healing stream flowing from Calvary's Cross; how wonderful it is that we may freely submerge ourselves in its restoring waters!

1. *Spirit-Filled Life Bible* (Nashville, TN: Thomas Nelson Publishers, 1991), 217, "Word Wealth: 15:25 make atonement."

2. Ibid., 1911, note on 2:22–25.

3. Ibid., 1032 "Kingdom Dynamics: Healing Prophesied Through Christ's Atonement."

4. Ibid., 1941, "Word Wealth: 2 health."

Lesson 7/Divine Healing and God's Will

GOD'S WILL TO HEAL BODILY AFFLICTION

In determining whether it is God's will to heal sickness or affliction, we have three lights to guide us. The first big light is the need, the second light is personal faith, and the third and most important light is the teaching of Scripture.

As we begin our study of divine healing and God's will, read Mark 1:40–44. This miracle account of the healing of a leper answers the question of whether it is Jesus' will to heal the sick. The leper has no problem with the power and ability of Jesus to heal his fatal disease; he said, "You can make me clean." But he, like many sincere people, was not certain that it was Jesus' will to heal him. His faith in the omnipotence of God resulted from his knowledge of the many healings Jesus was performing, so he was not asking whether it was His will to heal generally. But would He heal leprosy? And, more importantly, was He willing to heal him as an individual case? Jesus answered both questions, "I am willing; be cleansed"!

Here is a scriptural statement from the Savior declaring His willingness to heal even the most serious of diseases. Some, in rebuttal, will say, "But the leper's healing was only one case; how can you say that it applies to every case and every disease?" By way of answer, let it be noticed that Jesus' answer to the leper seemed to be a landmark response to the question of whether it was Jesus' "will" to heal. The question of will was recorded only once; Jesus' answer to the important question was "[Yes], I am willing!" Since we have no record of the question's arising again, it seems clear that Jesus was answering the question for all of us and that the Holy Spirit recorded it in the scriptures for our understanding and appropriation.

Be that as it may, Scripture answers the question unequivocally with Jesus' atoning work on the Cross. When Jesus, on the Cross, cried, "It is finished," He voiced the completion, once for all, of the atoning work of the Redeemer, which provided healing for both the soul and the body. The prophecy of Isaiah 53 and the statement of fulfillment in Matthew 8:16, 17 make it clear that the stream of vicarious atonement cleansed both the guilt of sin and the suffering of sickness for those who would believe. Jesus is always willing to heal, because His redemption applies to whosoever believes. When the lights of 1) Scripture ("I am willing" and "By His stripes we are healed"), 2) one's need of healing, and 3) one's God-given faith are in full alignment, one goes ahead to deliverance.

There are those who contend that all prayer must be accompanied by the proviso, "If it be Your will." Of course, it *is* true that our prayers should express our submission to God's will: "Your will be done" is in the prayer Jesus taught us. However, the supplying of needs based on the provisions of a covenant can be claimed by obedience to the covenant promise, because *the covenant itself is a statement of God's will.* In the Book of Exodus (15:26) God has given a healing covenant in which He reveals Himself as the Healer. His name is "the Healer"; and since "Healer" is one of His names, it reveals one of His attributes of nature. What God is by nature, He never ceases to be, for He has declared also, "I *am* the LORD, I do not change" (Mal. 3:6).

Just as with salvation, one of the conditions of being healed is believing:

"'But if You can do anything, have compassion on us and help us.' Jesus said to him, 'If you can believe, all things are possible to him who believes'" (Mark 9:22, 23). Since receiving healing requires positive faith, how can one exercise faith in a prayer that begins with an "If"? Would the Philippians, after receiving Paul's epistle, ever pray, "Lord, if it is your will please supply our needs"? Would the Romans ever pray after reading Romans 10:9, "Lord, I believe in my heart, and I have confessed with my lips my faith in your Resurrection; please save me, if it is Your will"? Would the Thessalonians, after reading Paul's first letter, pray, "We have read what your apostle said about your coming and about those who have died in the faith; now comfort our hearts, if it is Your will"?

Naturally we should pray reverently; and Jesus set a great

example for us in the Garden of Gethsemane when He prayed, "Father, if it is Your will, take this cup away from Me; nevertheless not My will, but Yours, be done" (Luke 22:42). However, when the Lord has given us a clear promise, let's not waver in faith when we ask for the promise's fulfillment by adding an "if." If an employer promised an employee a special bonus, wouldn't the employee show peculiar deference if not disrespect, to his employer if he said, "I have come to claim your promise *if you want to give it*"?

A scripture passage that is often quoted to support the idea that all prayers should be accompanied by the proviso "If it be Your will" is 1 John 5:14, "Now this is the confidence that we have in Him, that if we ask anything <u>according to His will</u>, He hears us." But this passage does not even suggest that we should pray with an "if." Whatever covenant promises we have, properly interpreted, are our privilege to claim. When we ask God for some blessing, we first determine that the blessing is clearly promised in Scripture, and second we make certain that we are fulfilling the conditions behind the promise. Since divine healing is a covenant promise, purchased by Christ's work of atonement, we need only assure ourselves that we have met the conditions.

Of course there are many complex situations in life about which one knows of no covering Bible promise. There are many general promises, the conditions for fulfillment of which we are unaware or do not recall. In all situations of life we desire to have the Lord with us, helping us through them. We ought to pray about everything; and when we are not certain about the will of God for the situation, it is altogether proper to ask for the revelation of His will. When we are confronted with a multiple-choice situation in which we have a preference, we certainly may ask God to implement our choice, but the prayer, indeed, should include, "If it be Your will."

ABOUT GOD'S GENERAL WILL AND HOW TO KNOW IT

This is a good place to discuss the broader subject of "the will of God." There are two categories of the will of God: 1) His general will, and 2) His specific will.

God's "general" will is clearly revealed in the Scriptures. If we want to know God's general will we must study the Scriptures systematically. Some people worry about whether they are living in the will of God. If one is a faithful student of the Bible, living up to all the light he has, he is for all practical purposes doing the general will of God. Regular Bible use develops our grasp of God's will, and we will progressively know and understand God's general will for life. Its contents have to do with morals, devotion, worship, service and communion.

For example, Paul makes reference in 1 Thessalonians to an inspired revelation establishing God's general will for Christian morality: "For this is the will of God, <u>your</u> <u>sanctification</u>: that you should abstain from sexual immorality" (1 Thess. 4:3). In other words, one does not have to ask God whether he can be unfaithful to his marriage vow; the Bible answers the question in "general" and that generality covers all specifics of immorality.

Another example: the general will of God, as delineated in the Scriptures, answers once and for all what the believer's attitude toward constituted government should be: "Therefore submit yourselves to every ordinance of man for the Lord's sake, whether to the king as supreme, or to governors, as to those who are sent by him for the punishment of evildoers and *for the* praise of those who do good. For <u>this</u> <u>is</u> <u>the</u> <u>will</u> of <u>God</u>, that by doing good you may put to silence the ignorance of foolish men" (1 Pet. 2:13–15).

However, knowing God's *general* will, we come to cases of seeking the specific will. God's specific will has to do with one's decisions and choices, such as where to go to school, whom to marry, what profession to follow, where to live, what church to be a part of, what people to have as close companions, what hobbies to have if any, what Christian service to choose, how much time to give to a chosen activity, how many children to have, what proportion of time to devote to work, home, church, community, and so on. God's specific will is illustrated in the following passage from Romans: "Making request if, by some means, now at last <u>I</u> <u>may</u> <u>find</u> <u>a</u> <u>way</u> <u>in</u> <u>the</u> <u>will</u> <u>of</u> <u>God</u> <u>to</u> <u>come</u> <u>to</u> <u>you</u>" (Rom. 1:10).

Knowing God's will for our lives is very important. This the apostle Paul makes very evident in a passage in Ephesians

5:15–17: "See then that you walk circumspectly, not as fools but as wise, redeeming the time, because the days are evil. Therefore do not be unwise, but <u>understand</u> <u>what</u> <u>the</u> <u>will</u> <u>of</u> <u>the</u> <u>Lord</u> <u>is</u>." If we are to walk wisely, making the most of all opportunities, it is essential that we know the will of God for our lives.

Knowing God's will was made important to Paul by the message of Ananias, through whom God chose to enlighten him concerning his miraculous conversion and his divine destiny: "Then he said, 'The God of our fathers has chosen you that you should <u>know</u> <u>His</u> <u>will</u>, and see the Just One, and hear the voice of His mouth" (Acts 22:14).

The discovery of God's will is much facilitated by overcoming conformity to the world's patterns: "And do not be conformed to this world, but be transformed by the renewing of your mind, that you may prove what *is* that good and acceptable and perfect will of God" (Rom. 12:2). When we have given ourselves wholly to God in consecration, walking in Christ's pattern, we demonstrate to ourselves in experience God's perfect will.

Advantages of knowing the will of God and walking in it are made evident by the following gems of Scripture. Write your observations about each verse's content as it bears on your life.

When we live as sincere servants of the Lord and not of men, we find ourselves doing God's will, not by coercion, but from the heart: "Not with eyeservice, as men-pleasers, but as bondservants of Christ, doing the will of God from the heart" (Eph. 6:6).

We can help one another know and walk in the will of God by interceding for one another in this regard: "For this reason we also, since the day we heard it, do not cease to pray for you, and to ask that you may be filled with the knowledge of His will in all wisdom and spiritual understanding" (Col. 1:9).

SOME ABC'S OF GOD'S WILL

A. The very first essential to learning God's will in any situation is the willingness to do God's will whatever it is. God will not show us His will so that we may think it over. If one is unwilling to do whatever God's will may be, the quest for the knowledge of it is an exercise in futility. We must pray, "Lord, show me Your will so I can do it," never, "show me Your will so I can consider it." Full surrender is the first step toward the discovery of the center of God's will.

Jesus expounded this principle to the religious leaders of His day who were arguing about what was God's will. He declared the following great truth: "If anyone wills to do His will, he shall know concerning the doctrine, whether it is from God or *whether* I speak on My own *authority*" (John 7:17). By "doctrine" Jesus does not have reference to formal theology, He was talking about His own teaching and life-style which the Father had given Him to share with the world: His teaching and behavior were God's will. He was saying that only those would understand His teaching who were obedient to His teaching. The Pharisees were unwilling to obey His truth; therefore, they could not comprehend it. They couldn't know God's will because they were unwilling to obey it.

B. The Holy Spirit is the believer's faithful guide in life; however, there will be times when it seems we may proceed by *"sanctified reason."* Mature Christians develop a spiritual sensitivity and intelligence that can be depended upon to guide them in the center of the Lord's way. Paul describes this mature judgment: "Brethren, I do not count myself to have apprehended; but one thing *I do*, forgetting those things which are behind and reaching forward to those things which are ahead, I press toward the goal for the prize of the upward call of God in Christ Jesus. Therefore <u>let us, as many as are mature, have this mind</u>" (Phil. 3:13–15). Read Acts 15:28 and see the blend of the Holy Spirit's wisdom applied by spirit-filled thinking.

C. Another pairing of instruments that will help to guide us in the will of God are "experience" and "circumstance." The more often that we experience God's will for our behavior or decisions, the easier it will be to find again the pattern of God's working. Then, in some cases our "circumstances" will point to God's will. There will be times when our circumstances will close us in to the degree that we have only one way forward. If that way is not outside God's *general will*, then you can be reasonably certain that the circumstances have been ordered by God's providence.

D. Another guide to God's will in a matter, is the advice of other believers. Read Proverbs 11:14 and 15:22. What does this indicate to you?

If several mature persons with experience in our matter of concern give us the same counsel, we can be reasonably certain that the counsel is good. In the early church God often revealed His counsel through the body—the church (Acts 13; 15).

WHY SOME PEOPLE WHO ARE PRAYED FOR ARE APPARENTLY NOT HEALED

If bodily healing is included in the Atonement, and Jesus has declared His willingness to heal, why is it that many sincere persons are not healed? This question is often asked as an earnest inquiry and other times as an unbelieving challenge. Let no one think we judge anyone as "less saved" if they either disbelieve in today's healing promise or if they believe in it but are not healed. The truth of the promise is not based on whether it is believed or sucessfully received. We simply proclaim this truth and leave the results to God, just as we witness or preach of Christ's salvation and leave the resultant decision for or against with Him.

Still, we humbly seek to discern and discover why some seek to receive healing and are not healed. Perhaps study of these insights may help you.

1. One of the most common reasons why those who are prayed for are not healed is failure to comply with the conditions (see Ex. 15:26). All God's promises are conditional. Read Psalm 1. Note God's promises of blessing and prosperity. What are the conditions being evidenced by the behavior of the blessed man? Note that blessing is denied to those who walk in ungodly counsel, who stand together with sinners, who occupy a seat of scornfulness. The person whom God blessed with health and prosperity was a person who delighted in doing the will of God and who had put behind him the life-style of the ungodly. The blessings of God were contingent upon a way of life that was worshipful and dutiful on the one hand and devoid of scornfulness or selfishness on the other.

2. Disobedience is another common reason why healing and other blessings may be denied. King Saul learned the lesson of obedience and the peril of disobedience when he rebelled against the counsel of God's appointed prophet Samuel. Study the incident, which climaxes with 1 Samuel 15:22, 23. See how disobedience brought an end to God's blessing on Saul.

PROBING THE DEPTHS

The contingency for participation in God's benefits is clearly set forth in Isaiah 55:2, 3. Note the key verbs.

Listen carefully to Me, and eat *what is* good,
And let your soul delight itself in abundance.
Incline your ear, and come to Me.
Hear, and your soul shall live;
And I will make an everlasting covenant with you—
The sure mercies of David.

In Hebrew the commands "Listen," "Incline your ear," and "Hear" are synonymous with "Obey." The covenant promise was "the sure <u>mercies</u> of David," which included bodily healing. When the blind man of Jericho cried out to Jesus requesting sight for his blind eyes, he phrased his urgent request with the words, "Son of David, have <u>mercy</u> on me!" He was aware of the covenant promise of Isaiah to bestow the "sure mercies of David." That Bartimaeus was prepared to live a life of obedience is seen in his conduct subsequent to his miraculous healing, "And immediately he received his sight, and <u>followed</u> <u>Him,</u> <u>glorifying</u> <u>God</u>. And all the people, when they saw *it*, gave praise to God" (Luke 18:43).

3. Some who pray for healing do not receive for lack of faith. The basic condition for bodily healing is "faith." In the ministry of Jesus, the healing of various persons was followed by His words, "Your faith has saved you" or "has made you well." (a) When the paralyzed man was brought to Jesus by lowering him through a hole made in the roof, it was said of Jesus, "When Jesus saw their faith . . ." (b) When the disciples could not cast out the evil spirit that possessed a young boy, they inquired of Jesus a reason for their lack of success. Jesus answered them, "Because of your unbelief." (c) When Jesus turned to the woman who had touched the hem of His garment, He assured her, "Be of good cheer, daughter, your faith has made you well."

Examine each of the following passages. How does each evidence "faith" as a condition for healing?

Mark 11:24

Acts 6:8

Acts 14:8–10

James 1:6, 7; 5:14–16

One might assume from the things said above about the importance of faith that unless one has extraordinary faith, it is useless to pray for healing. But it is simply the faith to pray that is essential. Since it is God who *gives* us faith, we should take all things to God in prayer without fearing that our faith is inadequate. Our sufficiency is in *Him* (2 Cor. 3:4–6).

4. Sometimes one's prayer is not answered immediately, because God is delaying the answer to teach a lesson. Something like this appears to lie behind the words of Paul to the Corinthians in 2 Corinthians 1:3–5. What does he say God will do while we are going through such delays?

If we do not receive an immediate answer to prayer for healing, we should not assume that God has not worked, nor that He will not answer fully.

5. James said, "You do not have because you do not ask." Sometimes, when we have a need, we *hope* that the Lord will fulfill the need, but we do not actually pray earnestly for the healing. We must not assume that we are merely God's "cosmic pets" and that He will just automatically give us all our secret or unspoken needs. Let us ask: 1) Have we actually gone to God in earnest prayer? 2) Have we called upon another to agree with us in prayer for healing? 3) Have we called for the elders of the church, asking them to anoint with oil and pray in unison? Why should we expect God to act when we have not laid the matter before Him in believing prayer? Let us heed the wisdom and promise James declares: "The effective, fervent prayer of a righteous man avails much" (James 5:16).

6. Sometimes prayer for healing is not effectual because there is some unconfessed sin that we must resolve. This must

be true, because in connection with the New Testament healing covenant we read: "Confess *your* trespasses to one another, and pray for one another, that you may be healed" (James 1:16). When guilt is simmering within us, faith is destroyed and without faith our praying is futile. Let us confess our sins to God on our knees. John wrote, "If we confess our sins, He is faithful and just to forgive us our sins and to cleanse us from all unrighteousness" (1 John 1:9). Faith readily fills a clean heart. Hidden guilt can be very deceptive. If faith seems dull, we might do well to search our hearts with the aid of the Holy Spirit to discover unconfessed sin, or the sin of unbelief.

7. A very destructive form of sin is unforgiveness. Prayer for healing may well go unanswered if we harbor in our hearts unforgiveness of another person. In the Sermon on the Mount recorded in Luke, Jesus taught us to pray, "And forgive us our sins, for we also forgive everyone who is indebted to us." To this, Matthew added, "For if you forgive men their trespasses, your heavenly Father will also forgive you. But if you do not forgive men their trespasses, neither will your Father forgive your trespasses" (Matt. 6:14). The sin of unforgiveness can too easily be overlooked, because we may view offenses as being the other person's fault. But our prayers will never be fully effective as long as hurts are unresolved.

8. Finally, God's providential oversight of our lives may be such that we will never understand why God's covenanted promises and provisions are not manifested in the way that we have understood them. God's wise providence is above our full comprehension. We can discover some of the reasons why everyone is not healed. However, no one should assume that they were not healed because it was not God's will.

Many persons who say, "It is not God's will to heal me," will quickly resort to every other avenue of recovery. So we might inquire, if you say it is not God's will for you to be healed, why do you make such effort to be healed by any means? But, of course, God *does* want people to be healed, and He heals by many means—including medical means. Let us cease doubting it is God's will to heal. If a believer feels more comfortable with medical or surgical therapy than with outright trust in divine healing, let him or her make that choice with no sense of guilt or failure. But let us ask for and trust in God's power and promise to heal. His presence is in the church, but also in the clinic or the operating room. Direct divine healing is a marvelous blessing, which believers should desire enough that before abandoning God's direct healing, they should explore every reason why it has not happened.

 ## FAITH ALIVE

The highest attainment of the Christian life is to live in the very center of God's will. We are helped to do this by following conscientiously the teachings of Scripture and by following the guidance of the Holy Spirit. We know from the clear teaching of such scripture passages as Exodus 15:26; Psalms 91, 103, 107; Isaiah 53; Matthew 8:5–17; James 5:13–18, that it is God's will to heal our sick bodies. That knowledge is verified by the many healings that happened in the ministry of the apostles, and it is fully illuminated by the fact of the undeniable presence of the Holy Spirit in the church of our day.

Since the Lord's provision is for the redemption of the total person—soul and body—it is our privilege and duty to appropriate for our lives the full measure of the Lord's provision, commensurate with our stage of maturation. If we can walk in the power of a Spirit-filled life, not only will our lives be blessed, but also our testimony will be soul-saving. The more God can do through our lives, the more we will be a blessing to others around us.

Almost all the persons Jesus healed during His earthly ministry went away rejoicing. If we can believe God's provision for healing, and experience it fully, not only will our lives be full of the joy of the Lord, but we will be instrumental in spreading joy to everyone we touch. "Always pursue what is good both for yourselves and for all. Rejoice always, pray without ceasing, in everything give thanks; for this is the will of God in Christ Jesus for you" (1 Thess. 5:15–18).

Lesson 8/Healing and the Spiritual Gift

The power of the Holy Spirit is infinite, immeasurable, and inexhaustible. The manifestation of the Holy Spirit's power in the church during the Christian era is beyond our reckoning. The sinners redeemed and transformed since the day of Pentecost by the Spirit's power cannot be numbered. The gospel ministries anointed by the Spirit would defy measurement. The Spirit's power, applied to energize all the countless answered prayers, no meter could measure. How could we calculate the Spirit's energy applied to recall God's precious promises? or to breathe out the total of divine revelation? or to inspire the human authors of Holy Scripture? or to expedite every creative act or sustaining force of God in all His universe? In spite of all the manifestation of the Spirit, His *still unused potential* is a greater outpouring of power than all the Niagaras in the world.

CONCERNING THE GIFTS OF THE SPIRIT

One of the works of the Holy Spirit is to equip believers for the work of ministering the gospel, discipling the converts, unifying the body of Christ, maturing the believers (Eph. 4:8, 11–13).

Who is the Giver of the gifts mentioned?

What are the ministry offices He gives? (v. 11)

What is the task of these ministries? (v. 12)

What is the goal of this task? (v. 13)

KINGDOM EXTRA

The Gifts Christ Gives. Distinguishing among the gifts of Romans 12:6–8 (from the Father), the gifts of 1 Corinthians 12:8–10 (from the Holy Spirit), and those in Ephesians 4:11, which are explicitly given by Christ the Son (v. 8), is pivotal in comprehending the whole scope of spiritual gifts.[1]

Now while there are many gifts of the Godhead listed in various Bible passages, most prominent are those in Romans 12:5–8, 1 Corinthians 12:1–31, and Ephesians 4:8–13; and while the different categories seem to be given severally by all three members of the Holy Trinity, it is the Holy Spirit's work to bring into manifestation all the gifts. For instance, the gifts of Ephesians 4 (ministry or person gifts), are declared to be gifts from Christ by virtue of His death and resurrection. However, Paul, speaking to the elders of Ephesus in Acts 20:28, reminds them that they were put into office by the ministry of the Holy Spirit. Paul, in Romans 12 (gifts from the Father), makes reference to some who have the gift of ruling (leadership), whose function according to Acts 20:28 would be by the work of the Holy Spirit. In 1 Corinthians 12:4–6, Paul mentions gifts, ministries, and activities issuing from the Spirit, the Lord, and God—the Trinity manifest in combined activity.

There are diversities of <u>gifts</u> [*charismata*], but the same <u>Spirit</u>. There are differences of <u>ministries</u> [Eph. 4], but the same <u>Lord</u>. And there are diversities of <u>activities</u> [Rom. 12], but it is the same <u>God</u> who works all in all (1 Cor. 12:4).

Since all of the above are about works of the Spirit (*pneumatika*, v. 1), all are enablements energized by the Holy Spirit. Verse 7 goes on to say "But the <u>manifestation of the Spirit</u> is given to each [of the above] for the profit *of all*."

Peter, speaking of the stewardship of the *charismata* in 1 Peter 4:10, 11, says:

> As each one has received a <u>gift</u>, minister it to one another, as good stewards of the manifold grace of God. If anyone speaks, *let him speak* as the oracles of God. If <u>anyone ministers, *let him do it* as with the ability which God supplies</u>, that in all things God may be glorified through Jesus Christ, to whom belong the glory and the dominion forever and ever. Amen.

Peter makes clear that gifts of great diversity are given to the church, to be operated in the power of the Holy Spirit. Since the work of the church is a supernatural work, it cannot be done by mere human talent. The Lord may use the latent talents, which believers have been given by nature, in His work, but He anoints that talent by the Spirit. How can this fact be of great comfort to believers? Jesus said to Peter and Andrew, "Follow Me, and I will make you fishers of men." And on the Day of Pentecost, Peter, the disciple of Jesus most prone to human errors, preached, in the power of the Holy Spirit, a sermon which won thousands of people to the Lord. Jesus made him a spiritual fisherman by praying the Father to send the "Comforter." The Holy Spirit is called the "Promise of My Father" (Luke 24:49), and is declared to be the gift of the Son (John 15:26; 16:7).

Write your own thoughts as to the way Peter's being so enabled holds promise for your own progress.

The gifts of the Spirit, enumerated in 1 Corinthians 12, appear to be gifts on which the word "manifestation" is emphasized. The Corinthians were active in and open to these supernatural gifts. All works of the Spirit are supernatural in character, but vary in the way they manifest or operate. In an operation of the Spirit, something is *done*.

- With some gifts, the object of the operation is simply the effect of the deed.
- In another, attention is called to the doing.
- With one kind of gift, a person may nurse a friend or loved one back to health with God-given skill and patience (the gift of helps, or showing mercy).
- With another kind of gift, the person may pray the prayer of faith with the words, "Rise, and walk!"

In the case of one, a supernatural caring is in operation; in the second, a supernatural recovery is manifested. But take note: the church has always had both kinds of gifts in operation; both kinds of gifts will always be needed in the ministry of the church.

Describe an instance of your sensing the Holy Spirit's using you to manifest His power through a gift operating. Don't be afraid to identify such occasions of grace-in-action.

WORD WEALTH

Manifest, manifestation, *phaneros, phanerosis.* "To make clear, visible, shining, open to sight, manifestation." Used only in 1 Corinthians 12:7; 2 Corinthians 4:2. In regard to the operation of a gift of the Spirit, "that which was visible, getting attention"; "calling attention to the presence of God's Spirit."

We have seen that God has provided many spiritual gifts for the church. Several lists are to be found in the New Testament. Since each list, gleaned from three different books, contains a different grouping of gifts, it is likely that the ones mentioned related to different needs and experiences of the particular churches. A number of Bible scholars are of the opinion that the New Testament lists do not exhaust all the possible gifted operations that the Lord may employ. It seems likely that there is a gift for every possible task that may be useful and edifying to the body of Christ. If there is a kind of work or ministry that God has put His blessing upon, there must be a gift to energize the ministry or work, for, as Peter states: "If anyone ministers, *let him do it* with the ability which God supplies, that in all things God may be glorified through Jesus Christ, to whom belong the glory and the dominion forever and ever" (1 Pet. 4:11).

THE OLD TESTAMENT TYPOLOGY OF SPIRITUAL GIFTS

Most New Testament blessings have their pattern given in an Old Testament typology. Examine Exodus 35:30–35, where the Old Testament pattern for spiritual gifts is found.

For every kind of skill or artistry needed for the construction of the tabernacle and its furnishings, for the making of all garments, curtains, priestly pertinences, and so on, skilled workmen were needed. In order that a large company of artisans could be trained, there had to be teachers. To accomplish this task, which was a divine project, God imparted the gifts needed for both the fabrication and the teaching by filling some with the Holy Spirit. The Spirit-filled men not only used their gifts of craftsmanship to make the articles, they used their gifts of teaching to train others. The whole project was carried out by gifted people, who, when the work was finished, gave all the glory to God.

Name the men appointed by Moses and the task each was given.

Note the divine resource each was given to accomplish his task. Write out the way the Word of God describes each one's enablements.

There is no way to exaggerate the importance of this "gifting." God gave to Moses the patterns of everything that would pertain to the worship, such as the tabernacle, the ark of the covenant, the altars, the table of showbread, the mercy seat, the priests' garments, the lampstand, lavers, and so on, all of which had to be crafted exactly according to the divine pattern: "And see to it that you make *them* according to the pattern which was shown you on the mountain" (Ex. 25:40). That the Old Testament tabernacle patterns were intended as a typology of New Testament fulfillments is seen from the reference to them in Hebrews 8:5: "Who serve the copy and shadow of the heavenly things, as Moses was divinely instructed when he was about to make the tabernacle. For He said, 'See *that* you make all things according to the pattern shown you on the mountain.'"

Do you think Jesus has a pattern for the "building" of His church? (Matt. 16:16–18) How do you think He plans to enable us who partner with Him to participate in this project?

THE REVEALED GIFTS

The Holy Spirit

The purpose for the discussion of gifts is to show that God has provided supernatural capacitation for the ministries of the church, ministries that were meant to abide and function in the church throughout the church dispensation. The very terms "Spirit-filled life" and "Spirit-filled church" assume the survival of all the spiritual gifts that were poured out on the church in the apostolic age. The idea that much of the church's original power was only needed "until the ecclesiastical train gained momentum" is absurd. In these latter times when the church is going uphill against increased opposition, the "Helper's" assistance—the Holy Spirit's power—is needed more than ever. However, whatever some may theorize, the gifts are still in operation. None of them is lost nor withdrawn.

First, let us take a brief look at the revealed gifts that seem to focus on the Holy Spirit's "giving" (1 Cor. 12:7–11).

1. *The Word of Wisdom.* We probably have an example of the exercise of this gift in the ministry of Stephen. Examine Acts 6:3, 8–10, and write the evidence that "wisdom" may well have been one of the gifts of the Spirit manifest through Stephen.

 WORD WEALTH

Wisdom, *sophia.* Practical wisdom, prudence, skill, comprehensive insight, Christian enlightenment, a right application of knowledge, insight into the true nature of things. Wisdom in the Bible is often coupled with knowledge (Rom. 11:33; 1 Cor. 12:8; Col. 2:3). In anticipation of our needing guidance, direction, and knowing, God tells us to ask for wisdom, assuring us of a liberal reception (James 1:5).[2]

2. *The Word of Knowledge.* The inclusion of the term *word* in the name of the gift does not necessarily mean that it is a vocal gift. The Greek word *logos* does not always mean a spoken word, it also has the meaning of "idea," "statement," "discourse," "subject matter." If a vocal gift had been intended, the word *rhema* would have been more apt. A scriptural description of this gift may be found in 1 Corinthians 1:5, "That you were enriched in every thing by Him in all utterance and all knowledge." If a "word of wisdom" gives insight to the church for practical action, a "word of knowledge" must

bring to light the principles of doctrine that form a basis for the action. This is the ideal gift for the anointed teacher.

Look at Acts 18:24–28. Who might be described as operating in this order of "teaching" knowledge?

What occurs in John 1:48–50; 4:17–18, and Acts 5:1–5 that might be described as an exercising of "revelatory" knowledge?

3. *The Gift of Special Faith.* Nearly all writers on spiritual gifts refer to this gift as that of "*special* faith." All of us become Christians by believing, by exercising "faith." But the faith behind this gift differs in degree and in application. This special faith is seen in action in the third chapter of Acts where Peter says to the lame man, "In the name of Jesus Christ of Nazareth, rise up and walk." It is seen again in Acts 14, where Paul says to another lame man, "Stand up straight on your feet." Special faith often works together with the gifts of "healings" and "workings of miracles."

Look up the two episodes mentioned (Acts 3:1—4:22 and 14:8–18). What was the cost to these leaders as a result of their exercising these gifts?

4. *The Gifts of Healings* are special anointings with which God enables members of the body of Christ to serve as instruments or vehicles by which God heals afflictions and restores wholeness to believers without the use of natural means. The healings may be physical, mental, emotional, or spiritual.

WORD WEALTH

Healing, *iamata.* "To heal" is used (a) of physical treatment twenty-two times; in Matthew 15:28 KJV, "made whole";

NKJV, "healed"; so also in Acts 9:34; (b) figuratively, of spiritual "healing," Matthew 13:15; John 12:40; Acts 28:27; Hebrews 12:13. First Peter 2:24 and James 5:16 have the word used in both the physical and spiritual sense. Luke the Physician uses the word fifteen times.

The name of this gift is unusual in several ways: 1) both words in the name are plural, and 2) the name is the only gift name that includes the word *charisma,* "gift," although all the gifts are *charismata* or "gifts of grace." It is not known certainly why this gift is plural in both terms "gifts" and "healings." Furthermore, the words are plural also in verse 28. The emphasis of the plurality of the words can mean that there are differing gifts of healing for different kinds of sicknesses and afflictions. It can also mean that each occurrence of healing is one gift; this latter could imply that the gifts are not given to persons as a fixed gift, but that the gifts are for the whole church and may be manifested at any time in answer to positive faith. It is very rare that anyone claims having the gift of healing. However, it is to be acknowledged that some New Testament people like Peter, John, James, and Paul were servants of the Lord through whom the gifts of healings were frequently manifested. There are, no doubt, in our time, persons whom God has called to a healing ministry, to whom He has given special faith.

5. *Operations of Miracles.* The gift to work miracles is given to the church. Anointed individuals, at providential moments, will be anointed to speak or act in the name of the Lord with supernatural results. In the New Testament, events of supernatural power are called "miracles, wonders, and signs" (Acts 2:22, 43; 6:8; 8:13). *Miracles* are "events of divine power"; *wonders* are "events that cause wonderment"; *signs* are "events that signify something." It is interesting that the word *wonder* is never used by itself. God never performs a miracle just to amaze or cause wonderment. God's wonders are always accompanied with a sign that "signifies something." Real miracles always glorify God and tell us something about God and His purposes.

Look up Acts 9:36–42 and Acts 13:8–12. Describe the miracles that occur, and name the parties involved.

6. *The Gift of Prophecy.* The word *prophet* comes from the Greek *prophetes,* which is derived from two words—*pro,* which means "before," "forth," "for," or "in behalf of"; and *phemi,* "to speak." The word *prophetes* can mean "one who predicts" (tells beforehand), "one who speaks forth," or "one who speaks for or in behalf of." Deuteronomy 18:18 gives a definition of the Old Testament prophet: "I will raise up for them a Prophet like you from among their brethren, and will put My words in His mouth, and He shall speak to them all that I command Him." There seem to be three levels of the prophetic gift in the New Testament:

1)A carryover of the Old Testament prophet (Agabus, Acts 11:28; 21:10, 11);
2)One with the "gift of prophecy" as the equivalent of "tongues and interpretation" (1 Cor. 14:5); and
3)Any anointed speaking that edifies, exhorts, or comforts (1 Cor. 14:3).

What was Agabus's prophecy? When was it fulfilled?

7. *The Gift of Discerning of Spirits.* "Discerning of spirits" comes from the Greek *diakriseis pneumaton,* "to discern, discriminate, or to distinguish." Paul used the word to reproach the careless Corinthians who had not "discerned" the Lord's body at the Lord's Supper (1 Cor. 11:29). This gift is not for the discerning of people, but the discerning of "spirits." Paul says, "Let two or three prophets speak, and let the others judge [discern of what spirit]" (1 Cor. 14:29). The biblical discernment of prophesyings was apparently not observed, so that Paul had to write to the Thessalonians not to "despise prophecies." Prophecy wisely disciplined was considered by Paul the most profitable of all the vocal gifts (1 Cor. 14:1).

Describe the instance of "discernment" surrounding Acts 8:23. Verses 1–25 tell the whole story. What resulted?

8 and 9. *The Gifts of Tongues and Interpretation.* This is literally "kinds of tongues." This could mean different languages or tongues of different application. According to 1 Corinthians 14:14–17, the one who speaks in tongues prays (v. 15), sings (v. 15), blesses (v. 16), and gives thanks (v. 17). Interpretation is needed in the assembly in order that the whole assembly can join in the praise and thanksgiving. Those who speak in tongues must pray for the gift of interpretation so that their gift's benefit may be shared with the assembly. Other uses of the gift of tongues: for inaudible praise to God, one's prayer language, and as a sign to an unbeliever (14:22).

The Father

"MOTIVATIONAL" or "CREATIONAL" Gifts Listed in Romans 12:3–8

These gifts seem to focus on Father God's creative work in each individual, in whom a different "mix" of the following will be given as a part of His Creator work in them. Thus, different people find their different "motivations" or inclinations according to God-given talents and skills (1 Cor. 12:6, 18).

1. Prophecy
2. Ministry (*diakonia,* service)
3. Teaching (spirit-anointed)
4. Exhortation (Heb. 10:25)
5. Giving—of one's own resources (Eph. 4:28)
6. Leadership (who stands before)
7. Showing mercy (kindness and compassion)

The Son

MINISTRY Gifts Listed in Ephesians 4:8–11
1. Apostles
2. Prophets

3. Evangelists
4. Pastors and Teachers

Assignment: Using a concordance, answer the following:

Name at least three "apostles" other than the original twelve.

Name at least three "teachers" identified in the New Testament.

Cite two references where pastors (also called bishops and elders) are mentioned.

Blending It All Together

The gifts which the Son of God has given are pivotal in assuring that the first two categories of gifts [Gifts of the Father and Gifts of the Holy Spirit] are applied in the body of the church. Ephesians 4:7–16 not only indicates the "office gifts" Christ has placed in the church along with their purpose. The ministry of these leaders is to "equip" the body by assisting each person: 1) to perceive the *place* the Creator has made him to fill, by His creative workmanship in him, and the possibilities that salvation now opens to his realization of what he was made to be; and 2) to receive the *power* of the Holy Spirit, and begin to respond to His gifts, which are given to expand each believer's capabilities *beyond* the created order and toward the redemptive dimension of ministry, for edifying the church and evangelizing the world.

In this light, we examine these clearly designated categories of giftings: the Father's (Rom. 12:6–8), the Son's (Eph. 4:11) and the Holy Spirit's (1 Cor. 12:8–10). While the study expands beyond those listings and beyond the above outlined structure of the gifts of the Godhead, this general outline will help in two ways. First, it assists us by noting the distinct interest and work of each member of the Trinity in providing for our unique purpose and fulfillment. Second, it prevents us from confusing our foundational motivation in life and service for God with our purposeful quest for and openness to His Holy Spirit's full resources and power for service and ministry.[3]

1. *Spirit-Filled Life Bible* (Nashville, TN: Thomas Nelson Publishers, 1991), 1792, "Kingdom Dynamics: The Gifts Christ Gives."

2. Ibid., 1636, "Word Wealth: 6:10 wisdom."

3. Ibid., 2023, "Kingdom Dynamics: Holy Spirit Gifts and Power."

Lesson 9/All in the Name of Jesus

For all of humankind for all the ages, the greatest of all names is the name of Jesus.

> God also has highly exalted Him and given Him the name which is above every name, that at the name of Jesus every knee should bow, of those in heaven, and of those on earth, and of those under the earth, and *that* every tongue should confess that <u>Jesus Christ *is* Lord</u>, to the glory of God the Father. (Phil. 2:9–11)

Many scholars identify Yahweh with the name *Jesus;* actually, the name *Jesus* is the Greek form of the Hebrew word that means, "Yahweh Saves." Companion names for our Redeemer are found in all parts of the Old Testament. One scholar T. C. Horton has found 365 names for the Savior—Jesus—one for every day in the year (*The Wonderful Names of Our Wonderful Lord* (Logos International, 1925). It is right and wise to research the riches of the name of Jesus, for it is *in His name* we are told that we as believers shall "lay hands on the sick, and they will recover" (Mark 16:18).

 PROBING THE DEPTHS

Names make a difference in the world of the Bible, and the most important names are those associated with our Savior. "You shall call His name JESUS, for He will save His people from their sins" (Matt. 1:21). "Jesus" is the Greek form of the Hebrew name "Joshua"; and both of them mean "The Lord Is Salvation."

There are hundreds of names and titles of Jesus Christ in the Bible, and each one is a dual revelation to us. It reveals what Jesus Christ is in Himself, and also what He wants to do for us. In *His Name Is Wonderful* (Tyndale House Publishers, 1985), Warren Wiersbe says that each name He bears indicates some blessing that He shares.

THE WONDERFUL NAMES OF JESUS

Names for Jesus begin with the Fall of man and his need of a Savior. In Genesis 3, the coming Redeemer is called the "Seed" of the woman, who would, in the "fullness of time" bruise the old Serpent's head.

Later in the Book of Genesis (49:10), we find another name of unusual interest: "The scepter shall not depart from Judah, nor a lawgiver from between his feet, until Shiloh comes; and to Him *shall be* the obedience of the people."

There is some uncertainty about the meaning and derivation of the word *Shiloh*, but study resolves questions and reveals a powerful truth.

   WORD WEALTH

Shiloh, *shiloh.* Shiloh was a city where the tabernacle was set up (Josh. 18:1). Here in Genesis it appears to be a proper name or title, which believers generally accept as a messianic designation of Jesus. The derivation is uncertain. One idea is that *shiloh* is a noun which means "the peaceful one." Another view is that *shiloh* is a noun with a pronominal suffix that should be understood to mean "his son"; thus, lawgivers and princes would not depart from Judah until his son comes. Another possibility is to divide *shiloh* into the two words *shay* and *loh,* which would mean "the one to whom tribute is brought." The most likely meaning of *Shiloh* is the one accepted by most of the ancient Jewish authorities who understood *shiloh* to be a word compounded from *shel* and *loh,* meaning "to whom it belongs." *Shelloh* may be expressed by the English phrases, "to whom it belongs," "whose is the kingdom," and "whose right it is to reign." See especially Ezekiel 21:27.[1]

Following through, we examine Ezekiel 21:27, which reads: "Overthrown, overthrown, I will make it overthrown! It shall be no *longer,* until He comes whose right it is, and I will give it *to Him.*"

Ezekiel's prediction is a messianic prophecy foretelling that the day when the failed rulers and leaders of a sinful world would give way to the advent of the "King of kings, and Lord of lords" who would establish His Kingdom of Peace and Righteousness. Thus, *Shiloh,* one of the oldest, earliest names prophesied regarding Christ, declares His *right* to reign. Praise His Name—He *deserves* to rule!

Most of the Old Testament prophets, through their telescopes of revelation, did not see the nearer coming of the Redeemer. They saw only Him who would bring the New Jerusalem. However, Isaiah, the great messianic prophet, saw Him in both roles as the ruling Lion as well as the redeeming Lamb.

Isaiah envisioned the virgin's Son who would be named Immanuel, "God-With-Us," the Child born whose four-tiered name would be "Wonderful, Counsellor" and "Prince of Peace," and at the same time would be the "Mighty God" and the "Everlasting Father." Consider all four of these names.

From every point of view from which one may contemplate Jesus, He is the Wonderful One. He is wonderful in power, wonderful in wisdom, wonderful in grace, wonderful in love; furthermore, He is wonderful in His Incarnation through which He manifested His love by identifying Himself with sin-benighted humankind as the atoning Sacrifice for their sinfulness and affliction.

Describe one way Jesus has worked a "wonder" in your life.

Jesus is the Counsellor who can guide His people through their dark and winding journey. Those who follow the wonderful counsel of the unerring Guide are no longer caused to stumble by "the counsel of the ungodly." Look up Psalm 32:8 and Isaiah 30:21, and describe two ways the Lord will counsel or direct us.

Jesus can provide the perfect redemption because He is also the Mighty God. He is mighty in "creation" (John 1:3), mighty in "revelation" (Heb. 1:1, 2), mighty in salvation (Eph. 3:16), mighty in works (Matt. 13:54), mighty in healing miracles (Rom. 15:19). Look up each reference and write your reflections on one of these.

Jesus is also the Everlasting Father. He never changes. His blessings will never expire nor be antiquated nor be unavailable. His healing and transforming miracles will follow those who believe as long as the "Good News" has not yet reached every nation, kindred, tongue, and tribe. Look up Hebrews 13:8, and apply to this name of His.

In a strife-ridden society, what a wonderful name of Jesus is Prince of Peace. Jesus left us a precious legacy of peace, recorded in John 14:27: "Peace I leave with you, My peace I give to you; not as the world gives do I give you. Let not your heart be troubled, neither let it be afraid."

Take time to pray over these names, and prayerfully partake of specific resources they offer. They are *all* "Jesus' name." List each, and beside it write a situation or person to which you would apply this name's power by faith.

SALVATION THROUGH THE NAME OF JESUS

To Isaiah He was also seen to be the "Man of sorrows and acquainted with grief," by whose sacrificial death He would become the "wounded" One "for our transgressions," and the "bruised" One "for our iniquities [sicknesses]." Isaiah's parents were guided by the Holy Spirit in naming him "Isaiah," which means, "Yahweh Is Salvation." He was to be the prophet who would herald the coming of the "suffering servant of Yahweh," who was named "Jesus" because He would "save His people from their sins" (Matt. 1:21). That it was Jesus whom Isaiah saw is proved beyond doubt by the words of Jesus in John 12:38–41, which passage is concluded with the sentence: "These things Isaiah said when he saw His glory and spoke of Him."

Many people have the wrong notion that salvation in the Old Testament was attained by the keeping of the Law of Moses. This is not true. Rather, the Law of Moses was given as a standard by which an orderly society or theocracy might be maintained.

God gave the Law, not to save man from sin, but to make man aware of his sin. The requirements of the Law were such that man, with his sinful nature inherited from Adam and Eve, could not possibly observe it fully. Usually, when people read the Law carefully, they repented in sackcloth and ashes.

When Adam sinned, he was driven from Eden and taught that he could approach a Holy God only by means of a sacrifice (Gen. 3:15, 21; 4:4). When Abraham was commanded to slay his son Isaac on Mt. Moriah, he obeyed. According to Hebrews 11:17–19, why was Abraham willing to sacrifice Isaac? What was the promise gained and the lesson learned when God intervened? (Gen. 22:10–14)

This principle of a promised, necessary substitute was further taught by the Mosaic system. In Israel, the High Priest entered the Holy of Holies (Mercy Seat) once every year to make an atonement for the sins of the people. The death sentence was transferred to the blemishless animal, freeing the redeemed person to approach God. Naturally, an animal could not, in effect, substitute for a sinful person. The slain lamb was only a type of the infinite Lamb of God, who in the "fullness of time" would die for all sinners who would call upon God in faith. He who would come was the One believed for and by whom Old Testament believers would be saved. Jesus did this as very God, by whom all things were created. As the Lamb of God, He died on the Cross, arose from the dead, and ascended to the right hand of the Father, and now remains forever our Great High Priest. Through Him we come boldly to the throne of grace in His name. "To Him all the prophets witness that, through His name, whoever believes in Him will receive remission of sins" (Acts 10:43). Thus, all access to God—for both Old Testament and New Testament believers—is through our perfect and eternal Mediator.

Approaching God's throne in the name of Jesus means that we go before God just as if it were Jesus making the approach. This is why Jesus said to us, "And whatever you ask *in My name,* that I will do, that the Father may be glorified in the Son. If you ask *anything in My name,* I will do *it*" (John 14:13).

How did Jesus come to have the name above all names? (Phil. 2:6–11)

How did Jesus' disciples come to know every place where Jesus was revealed in the Old Testament? (Luke 24:25–27)

Give four names of Jesus found in the book of Isaiah.

What are the dynamic meaning and implications in the name *Shiloh*?

How were people "saved" in the Old Testament?

HEALING IN THE NAME OF JESUS

Having studied the meaning and power inherent and resident in Jesus' name as prophesied, let us look at His commission to us to go and heal the sick.

When Jesus sent out the seventy whom He appointed to announce the kingdom of God, He said to them, "And <u>heal the sick</u> there, and say to them, 'The kingdom of God has come near to you'" (Luke 10:9). When they returned from their preaching tour, they reported: "Lord, even the demons are subject to us <u>in Your name</u>." And He said to them, "I saw Satan fall like lightning from heaven" (Luke 10:17, 18).

 KINGDOM EXTRA

The Disciples Instructed to Heal. Jesus' instructions to the seventy sent out in the surrounding countryside are direct and clear: "Heal the sick there and say to them, 'The kingdom of God has come near to you.'" The coming of God's kingdom and the ministry of healing are not separated. The same point is made with the 12 disciples in Luke 9:1, 2. The authority to heal has been given to Jesus' disciples as they are willing to exercise the privilege of being messengers and participants in the kingdom of God. This ministry should not be divided from the complete declaration of the coming of the kingdom. The Holy Spirit delights to confirm the presence of the kingdom by glorifying the King's power, verifying Jesus Christ's working through the ministry of healing. This ministry of healing is experienced throughout the whole of the Book of Acts, and in James 5:13–16 is declared to be one of the responsibilities of eldership in a local congregation.[2]

One of the first notable miracles of healing in the name of Jesus in the ministry of the apostles after Jesus' ascension, is recorded in Acts 3:2–7. Read this passage and note (a) the disciples' perception, (b) their response to the need, and (c) the three steps in their ministering of healing.

The result of the healing of the lame man was immediate. The news of it reached the whole city. The disciples were soon surrounded by multitudes who wanted to know how the great miracle happened. The lame man was apparently well known by everyone because he daily begged at the gate of the temple. Some people began to assign miracle power to the disciples. Read verse 16 and record Peter's response.

The next day the apostles were called by the religious leaders and rulers to give an account of how they had healed the lame man, causing great excitement to the whole city. Peter, who once in fear denied his Lord, spoke boldly to the council. What was the core of his explanation as to how the man was healed? (Acts 4:9, 10)

The apostles attributed the healing power to Jesus and the declaration of His name. Their only part was to respond to the Holy Spirit, who gave them special faith, and to speak the words in Jesus' name which the Spirit gave to them. They had denied that the miracle was in any way related to any power or godliness of their own. They were good men, but it was the righteousness of Jesus and the name of Jesus to which the miracle had to be attributed. What might you conclude as to your privilege, given such a setting?

After the stoning of Stephen (Acts 7), there arose a fanatical persecution of the whole church, driving many out of Jerusalem. Among those who fled Jerusalem was Philip, who arrived in Samaria and soon began to preach. In the New Testament, Philip is designated as an evangelist. An evangelist specializes in preaching the Gospel of Christ with the aim to win souls for Christ, but often such preaching is attended by signs and wonders. Read Acts 8:4–8, 12 and list the kinds of things that happened.

Afterward, Philip was led by the Spirit to witness to one person traveling through the desert. The evangelist to the multitudes was just as skilled in personal witnessing. He won the eunuch, preaching Jesus to him from the Book of Isaiah. Some believe that the Ethiopian treasurer carried the gospel back to his land, which then became a strong Christian nation. Philip had power in witnessing to many or to one; his message was Jesus—his preaching and prayers made mighty through the wonderful name of Jesus.

Our study of the *name of Jesus* returns us once again to the New Testament healing covenant in James 5:13–18. The covenant has two parts: the part of the sick person, and the part of the elders who pray. 1) The sick are to call for the elders; 2) the elders are to anoint the sick with oil and to pray over them. Read the text and describe exactly *how* the elders are to pray: (a) doing what? (b) in what? (c) with what kind of prayer?

Anointing with oil was done to indicate that the power to heal came from the Holy Spirit and not from the elders who prayed. Prayer in the name of Jesus was uttered to affirm that Jesus, whose name is above every name, is the Mediator who has given all who believe access to the throne of grace. The sick may need to confess sins, make amends, pray one for another; but when everything that hinders faith is removed, and God is approached through our High Priest "by whose stripes [we] were healed, the prayer of faith will save the sick" (James 5:16). Of this we are assured by Him who promised, "If you ask <u>anything</u> in My <u>name</u>, I will do *it*" (John 14:14).

In the beginning of this chapter, reference was made to the prophet Isaiah's predictions about the coming of the "Servant" of Yahweh. The prophet called attention to the extraordinary significance of several of the names of the Messiah. In chapter 42, He is called both "Servant" and "The Elect [Chosen] One" in whom the Father "delights." That delight is derived from the fact that His "Servant" would become the "Light to the Gentiles" nations. In Matthew 12:15–23, this passage from Isaiah is quoted.

Jesus warned the people not to publicize the healings, because He was not yet ready to rule upon the throne of David; that would come later. Now He must reveal His blessing that would flow from His great heart of love, such as pardon from sin and healing of the afflicted. He had come to suffer and to die and, thereby, provide our redemption. If His healings out of compassion became too widely heralded, the people would demand for Him a crown and royal robe; He is now "the Lamb of God"; later He will be the "Lion of the Tribe of Judah."

This now is the age for reaching the nations with the message of redemption; this is the era in which the gospel, the message of access to the Mercy Seat of God, through the *name* of Jesus, must be declared to all. One could say that this is the dispensation of "The Name." Access in the name, forgiveness through the name, healing in the name, all prayer answered in the name—this is the blessing of the age of *grace*. Matthew wanted the readers to know that there would be a dispensation when all the nations would put their trust in One who would humbly suffer for their salvation of soul and body, for the total person. Blessed be the name!

 FAITH ALIVE

Conclude the chapter by writing a personal praise psalm to Jesus—extolling *the beauty of, the promise in,* and *the power through* Jesus' name. You need not be self-conscious as to rhyme or writing skill; simply allow the Holy Spirit to overflow your heart with words of faith-inspiring praise and exaltation.

1. *Spirit-Filled Life Bible* (Nashville, TN: Thomas Nelson Publishers), 1991, 77, "Word Wealth: 49:10 Shiloh."
2. Ibid., 1532, "Kingdom Dynamics: The Disciples Instructed to Heal."

Lesson 10/Healing in the Ministry of Jesus

Jesus made promise to two or three in agreement, and healing to those with persistent faith. In this chapter we will examine many of the healing miracles of Jesus with the aim of learning from Him more of how He goes about transmitting the healing blessing.

The dictionary defines a *miracle* as "an extraordinary event manifesting divine intervention in human affairs; an extremely outstanding or unusual event, thing, or accomplishment." Some people who deny the existence of miracles think of them as happenings that would violate the laws of nature. However, what we call the "laws of nature" are only our very limited understanding of nature. If God created all of nature, then what we call "laws of nature" are only the result of our very finite study and observation. God never has to violate any laws, because it is His universe and His unusual workings and manifestations will only be understood by, and available to, His believing children. The more we embrace the Living Word, and live by the written Word, the more we will experience the Lord's unusual operations.

Examine the following passages of scripture and note the different words which are used to describe the miraculous or wondrous.

John 4:48

Acts 2:19, 22, 43

Acts 4:30

Acts 7:36

Acts 14:3

Romans 15:19

2 Corinthians 12:12

Hebrews 2:4

The Bible uses several words to describe unusual, divine happenings. The terms *miracle, sign,* and *wonder* refer to that which attracts attention, causes amazement and admiration. The terms *powers* and *works* describe divine operations that do not necessarily attract attention, but accomplish divine purposes beneath the surface. *Signs* are visible, attracting attention; however, they also tell us something about the meaning of the event. In the New Testament the term *wonder* never appears by itself; it is always accompanied by *sign* or *miracle* (signs and wonders).

God never does amazing things just to attract attention, or to satisfy curiosity. When God amazes us with a miracle, which He often does, it is always that He may teach or reveal to us truth about Himself or His way of working with us. When a lame man jumps to his feet and walks in answer to prayer, that is a miracle wonder; when a leper is gradually healed as he goes to show himself to the priest, that is a divine work and a miracle, because leprosy was thought of as incurable. If a person is given word that a treatment may cure his condition in three months, and he is fully restored in a week, that is a work of divine power, but probably would not be called a miracle because of its gradual working.

Give a definition of a miracle in your own words.

What words are used in the New Testament to describe supernatural events?

How does a "sign" differ from a "wonder"?

What two New Testament words for a divine operation do not necessarily cause outward wonderment?

How can God work in our lives without causing us amazement?

JESUS CALLED TO HEAL A RULER'S SON

Begin by reading John 4:46–51. Make a simple outline of the passage.

Jesus' first recorded miracle was His turning water into wine at a marriage in Cana. On His return to Cana of Galilee, He was called upon for the healing of a nobleman's (ruler's) son who was sick in Capernaum, a city on the Sea of Galilee about 16 miles east of Cana. Capernaum was an important city, with a seat of government. Jesus devoted much of His ministry to Capernaum.

Growing Faith in Your Family

It is worthy of note that Jesus was often called upon to minister to family members of the supplicant. It is important for parents to teach their children to trust in God and to look to Him as a source of health and healing in answer to believing prayer. Even when family sickness seems to require the presence of a physician, the Great Physician should be invited to assist and to overshadow the family doctor. Every good doctor knows that his procedures will work only because the Lord our Maker has built into all of us a healing capacity. The prayer of faith will make any procedure work better.

The nobleman besought Jesus earnestly to go to Capernaum to heal his son. Jesus met the nobleman with a mild rebuke, a faith-testing reprimand. The religious ruler represented the Jewish nation, prone to believe only when "signs and wonders" were present. The nobleman met the test and he continued to beseech Jesus earnestly. Jesus gave him a second test by saying to him, "Go your way; your son lives."

Receiving Jesus' Promise Without "Seeing"

The nobleman expected Jesus to go with him to pray for his son. To return home with only a word of promise demonstrated his faith in Jesus. He believed in Jesus' word. Many people say, "I could believe in healing if I ever saw a real miracle." People who will not believe the Word of God will never really believe. Visible miracles may strengthen our faith in God's promises, but they will never be sufficient alone to give us true faith for healing. Peter said, "Whom having not seen you love. Though now you do not see *Him,* yet believing, you rejoice with joy inexpressible and full of glory" (1 Pet. 1:8).

What basic lesson do you find in this case study from Jesus' ministry?

THE HEALING OF A ROMAN SOLDIER'S SERVANT

Read Matthew 8:5–13. What single fact most impresses you in this passage?

A Seeking Society

Roman centurions in the New Testament record are usually men of high caliber and of admirable character. (See Matt. 27:54; Acts 10:1, 2; 21:32; 22:25, 26; 23:17, 18; 24:23; 27:6, 43; 28:16.) This centurion, like many educated Romans, had ceased to believe in the gods and goddesses of pagan Rome. They had come to see the greater logic in monotheism over polytheism. Many Gentiles of that era had become proselytes to Judaism, or at least proselytes of the gate.

A Surprising Seeker

This centurion was also greatly honored by Jesus, who marvelled at his qualities. He has been called "the man who surprised the Lord."

- He was surprising in his *humanity* (he loved his sick servant; most Roman slave masters would have left a sick slave to die).
- He was surprising in his *devotion* (he loved the Lord's people; most Romans hated the ever-rebellious Jews).
- He was surprising in his *generosity* (he built the Jews a synagogue with his own money).
- He was surprising in his *humility* (the Jewish leaders, who sent him to Jesus, declared that he was worthy of healing help; the centurion considered himself unworthy to have Jesus enter his home).

- He had surprising *insight into principles of authority* (he compared Jesus' authority over nature to his over his soldiers; thereby he was able to conceive of Jesus' power to heal by a word of command).
- He surprisingly understood that *one only understands authority* over others when he has submitted to authority.
- He had surprising *faith* (greater than anyone in Israel, since the psalmist said, "He sent His Word and healed them"). While the centurion did not receive Jesus into his house, he did receive Him into his heart and life.

For us, Jesus has already spoken His word of healing; we need but to ask, to believe, and to receive. Lord, give us faith like that of the centurion!

How does the New Testament represent the character of Roman centurions?

How did the centurion reason that Jesus could heal his servant with just a word?

What principle do you find in this case of Jesus' healing ministry?

HEALING IN THE FAMILY

"Now when Jesus had come into Peter's house, He saw his wife's mother lying sick with a fever. So He touched her hand, and the fever left her. And she arose and served them" (Matt. 8:14, 15).

A Healing Presence

Here is a healing miracle in which Jesus took the initiative. Upon entering Peter's house, He observed a sick woman, the mother of Peter's wife. Out of compassion He stretched forth His hand to apply the healing touch. *One cannot help drawing from this story the thought that to have Jesus in our homes is to live with the healing presence.* In a time when society is to some extent abandoning family values, the church and all Christian people must hold fast in defense of the home as the God-given institution for the perpetuation of the society. What a blessing it is to be a part of a family where Jesus is a constant guest!

A Healing Touch

It is worthy of notice that Jesus healed Peter's mother-in-law by touching her hand. She immediately arose and began to serve. For people who serve, the hands are of highest importance. Jesus not only restored her health, He restored her ability to serve, which was probably not only her greatest capability, but also her greatest pleasure.

Nothing in life brings a greater reward, both here and hereafter, than the service of others. In another story a woman touched Jesus and was healed. Here Jesus touched the woman and she was healed. In James 5 the elders lay hands upon the sick, and they are healed. The touch must be an aid to faith. In the first two stories the sick persons were healed from a distance by a word from Jesus. There are many avenues to healing; faith is the essential ingredient.

What means of healing's transmission is focused here?

What principle might we draw from the way Jesus took the initiative in Peter's home?

THE HEALING OF THE DEMON-POSSESSED

The Reality of the Demonic

Demon possession is not a pleasant subject; and some even deny the existence of demon spirits. But there is no way we can overlook demons. Jesus believed in their existence and healed many who were tormented by them. Some say that Jesus was only accommodating His speech to the beliefs of His day. But Jesus came to reveal the truth; in fact, He is Truth itself. Furthermore, if the Bible is God's Word for all ages, Jesus would not have perpetuated a human superstition to be read through the centuries. In our day, as occult teachings sweep the world, it is no time to deny what Jesus taught about Satanic beings. Increasing manifestations of evil are surfacing in our time, which cannot be accounted for apart from acknowledging the activity of evil spirits.

Jesus spoke of Satan and of evil spirits. He sent His disciples out with power over demon spirits; they returned rejoicing that the demon spirits were subject unto them in Jesus' name. All the four Gospels contain accounts of the casting out of demon spirits. Read the account in Matthew 6:28–34.

The Release of the Demoniacs

These demon-possessed men were so violent that their habitat was avoided by the public. When Jesus passed by, the demons recognized His lordship over all and cried out. They feared that Jesus had come to cast them out of the men. Loathing disembodiment, they requested to be cast into a herd of pigs. The texts do not say that Jesus cast the spirits into the pigs; He merely released their hold on the human victims, permitting them to go where they could. They chose the pigs.

The man out of which the demons were cast requested the permission to follow Jesus. Jesus commanded him to go back to his country and to evangelize, to tell his story of freedom from demon control. This he did with great success, for people received his testimony of Jesus' Person and power. Lesson: The church must rededicate itself anew to spiritual warfare against Satan's oppression with the weapon of prayer. What revival could come if thousands could be released from the evil spirits and influences that motivate them! Make personal notes on Jesus' procedure in dealing with the demons' debates (abrupt) and the demoniac's bondage (how He delivered him).

JESUS RAISING THE DEAD

Matthew 9 records the story of the raising of the daughter of Jairus, a ruler of the synagogue. Read Matthew 9:18, 23–26. Outline the essential details.

Dealing with a Textual Question

In the accounts in Mark and Luke, the father is represented as saying that his daughter was at the point of death. There is no contradiction really. When the ruler left his home, the daughter was at the point of death. Jairus (Matthew does not give his name) had expressed both conditions to Jesus. On the way to the house of Jairus, Jesus had delayed to heal the woman who touched the hem of His garment (Matt. 9:19–22); when He arrived at the ruler's house, his daughter had already died. Jesus said to the family, "She is not dead, but sleeping." Jesus had said the same to Mary and Martha where there was no doubt of Lazarus's actual death. In other words, there is no question the girl was dead, not merely comatose. In several places in Scripture, the death of those in Christ is represented figuratively as sleep (1 Cor. 15:51; 1 Thess. 4:14). Both Mark and Luke state that when Jesus prayed for her, "her spirit returned."

Determining Christ's Dominion Over Death

Jesus raised several from the dead. There were Lazarus (John 11) and the son of the widow of Nain (Luke 7), besides the daughter of Jairus. In Peter's ministry, Dorcas was raised from the dead (Acts 9:36–42). In Paul's travels Eutychus was raised from the dead after falling from a window during a long sermon (Acts 20:7–12). Paul himself, after being stoned at

Lystra, was apparently raised up through the prayers of his companions in the faith, having been left for dead at the point of his stoning (Acts 14:19, 20).

On the occasions that Christ brought back people from the dead, these were not true resurrections so much as a restoration to life, as there is no indication that these people were other than returned to the life that they had left. In other words, they did not live forever—they eventually died natural deaths. Paul tells us explicitly that Christ is "the first fruits of those who have fallen asleep" (1 Cor. 15:20). Still, these miracles show us Christ as supremely the master of this and any other situation in which death's power inflicts itself on human organs, families, businesses, or bodies.

These accounts of the raising of the dead demonstrate to us that Jesus, who Himself arose from the dead, is the Prince of life, the giver of eternal life. Although each of those mentioned above finally died a natural death, Jesus arose never to die. Let us have no doubt about living again, for we are already seated together with Christ in heavenly places (Eph. 2:1–7).

What promise do you derive from this point of study?

Have you ever heard testimony of a person restored from death? If you did, what would incline you to believe or disbelieve it?

 FAITH ALIVE

Read Matthew 15:22–28. Seeing this case in which Jesus does not at first respond (because He was not yet ministering to Gentiles), answer:

What can we learn about persistence?

What do we see of Jesus' overriding compassion?

What was the quality that prompted Jesus' response?

How difficult does deliverance from demons appear when faith is present?

A study of Jesus' miracles of healing should strengthen our faith to believe that His love and power are unchanging and available to all who have need.

Lesson 11/Healings in the Book of Acts

Lois was five, a little bright-eyed child who often bore the brunt of other children's meanness for one reason. It was earlier in this century, and she was the daughter of Pentecostal evangelists. It wasn't unusual for scorn and scoffing to assail these pioneers of faith whom time would later certify as sound-minded, Bible-centered, Christ-exalting believers.

But it wasn't meanness this day—only an accident— when she was innocently pushed backward by a neighbor boy into a tub of boiling water in which the family washing was soaking. When Lois screamed in pain, the woman of the house who was entertaining the evangelists pulled her from the boiling tub. Since they were in the countryside, far from a town, her relatives and the host gathered around Lois and prayed in agreement that God would heal her; some of the group fasted and prayed for several days.

The little child was covered with blisters, some of which observers said would hold a cup of water. Many of the neighbors were critical of the evangelists for not finding a way to get her to a hospital or physician, though distance and unfamiliarity with the area were factors and modern burn units were an unknown thing in that day. Some who were knowledgeable predicted that she would never walk again; others said, "She will be scarred for life." Confessedly, under normal circumstances, a physician should have been consulted; however, the die had been cast, and the family tended lovingly in care and prayer.

It was about a week later that little Lois awoke—the child's heart rising with a wellspring of faith that no human could beget. "I am going to walk in the name of Jesus," she said, and she rose from her bed, began to walk, and from that instant recuperated with amazing and total recovery, with not one scar from the awful burn. The news of the healing reached far and wide; hundreds who had heard of the healing came to the evangelists' meetings and many accepted Christ. This episode is true—the testimony of my (Nathaniel Van Cleave's) wife who now, in her 80s, is a healthy, constant witness to the love and grace of God.

As we turn to the Book of Acts for a study of healing events there, we begin with this testimony. The reason? The Book of Acts might only be studies in the awareness that it is only the beginning of fulfilled promise which continues to this day. The promise is Christ's: "And these signs will follow those who believe . . . they will lay hands on the sick, and they will recover . . . And they went out and preached everywhere, the Lord working with *them* <u>confirming</u> the word through the accompanying signs" (Mark 16:15–20).

WORD WEALTH

Confirming, *bebaioo.* To make firm, establish, secure, corroborate, guarantee. The miracles that accompanied the disciples' preaching confirmed to the people that the messengers were telling the truth, that God was backing up their message with supernatural phenomena, and that a new dispensation, the age of grace, had entered the world.[1]

KINGDOM EXTRA

"Many scholars question the authenticity of [Mark 16:9–20] primarily because of omission of these verses in some of the earliest manuscripts, and because their style is somewhat different from the rest of Mark. However, Christian writers of the second century, such as Jusin Martyr, Irenaeus, and Tatian testify to the inclusion of these verses, and the earliest translations, such as the Latin, Syriac, and Coptic, all include them. In any case, the passage does reflect the experience and expectation of the early church concerning the practice of charismatic gifts, and the question of its authenticity should remain open."[2]

Acts is a procession of miracles confirming Jesus' promise! Immediately after the account of the Spirit's outpouring on the Day of Pentecost (Acts 2), we read, "Then fear [reverent awe] came upon every soul, and many wonders and signs were done through the apostles" (Acts 2:43). Worthy of note is that the Greek preposition emphasizes "through the apostles," not "by the apostles" (*dia* not *huper*). From there, Acts 3 immediately relates the healing of the lame beggar at the Beautiful Gate, a miracle of healing from which repercussions continue through Acts 4. From this point, the healings and miracles in Acts may be broadly placed in four divisions: Healings 1) among multitudes, 2) through Philip, 3) through Peter, and 4) through Paul.

HEALINGS AMONG MULTITUDES

Following the Pharisees' attack after the healing of the man at the Beautiful Gate—being strictly warned and threatened by the rulers—the church gathered to pray for new boldness and a new outpouring of the Spirit accompanied by healing miracles. God answered their prayers abundantly as shown by a passage in Acts 5:12–16. Read this passage and answer the following questions:

What was the spiritual atmosphere here?

What different types of miracles occurred?

What were the responses of the people?

What unusual type miracle occurred?

What were the evangelistic results?

The faith of the church and of the people arose to such heights that practically every sick person was healed. The text does not say that the shadow of Peter was a healing technique of the apostles; the power of God was present to the degree that the people believed they would be healed whether Peter laid hands on them or not. Many people in our time have testified to being healed instantly while sitting in a seat listening to the ministry of the Word.

The Bible describes so many ways of receiving answers to prayer, that we must conclude that "faith" is the essential ingredient. However, there are many actions that are aids to faith, such as holding hands in agreement, the laying on of hands, the anointing with oil, anointed handkerchiefs, and so on. We ought not to put an exaggerated trust in outward gestures, but if they assist faith, it isn't unacceptable to use them, while looking to Jesus, the Great Physician, for the deliverance.

What aids to faith have you found helpful in receiving answered prayer?

What Scripture episodes can you think of that mention actions that helped people to healing or answered prayer? (examples to check after you've answered: 2 Kin. 4:3; 2 Kin. 20:7; Mark 2:4; Acts 19:12; James 5:14–16)

HEALING THROUGH THE MINISTRY OF PHILIP

The first church deacons were taken from among those who had evident faith and wisdom. Two of them had a ministry of healing. Stephen was martyred for his bold faith, and

Philip became an evangelist whose ministry God greatly honored. Acts 8:5–8 describes his ministry in Samaria. Read that passage and respond:

What significance do you see in the fact Samaria was being ministered to? (Compare Luke 9:51–56; 10:25–37; John 4:1–30.)

What kind of miracles occurred?

What was the social impact of the revival?

In Philip's healing ministry, two kinds of healings are given special mention. Many were delivered from evil spirits. Demon possession is very common where pagan worship is almost universal. The condition exists today in proportion to the false and occult religions in an area. Missionaries tell that in Sri Lanka almost everyone who comes to Christ has to be delivered from evil spirits. Missionaries in Colombia have told of the same fact. With the swelling of evil in our land today, demon bondage and oppression increase. Describe the power of the Gospel over demon spirits in the following passages:

Matt. 10:1

Matt. 12:28

Mark 1:21–25

The lame and the paralyzed were healed in large numbers in Philip's Samaritan ministry. It is not clear whether palsy was a more common malady of that area, or that Philip had special faith to pray for the paralyzed. The healing of one paralyzed would attract more attention than interior maladies. It appears that the healings attracted great crowds, and multitudes accepted Christ. Philip's ministry to the Samaritans marked a step forward in the progress from Judaism to a gospel for the whole world, the Samaritans being a mixed race of Jewish and Gentile blood. Philip's success was an extension of the seed Jesus had planted in Samaria, and an evidence of overcoming ethnic disharmony through the love of God.

HEALING THROUGH THE MINISTRY OF PETER

Jesus prophesied that He would endue His disciples with Holy Spirit power and make them witnesses, step by step, to the whole world: "But you shall receive power when the Holy Spirit has come upon you; and you shall be witnesses to Me in Jerusalem, and in all Judea and Samaria, and to the end of the earth" (Acts 1:8). The apostles had established a foundation in Jerusalem; Philip had evangelized Samaria. Now the time came that the gospel must extend to the Gentiles. Persecution had driven the apostles out of Jerusalem toward Roman areas, and soon God would transform Saul of Tarsus into an apostle to the Gentiles. But Peter would be used of God to make the first advance to the Romans. Peter's stops at Lydda and Joppa were the first on a journey that would lead to Caesarea and to the house of a Roman named Cornelius.

Healing at Lydda

While in Lydda (Acts 9:33–35) Peter found a paralyzed man in need of Christ. Describe what happened.

Aeneas was well-known in Lydda (modern Lod) as one afflicted. With his healing, the news of the gospel spread far and wide. Luke writes that all of Lydda and Sharon were converted as God used a healing miracle to open the door to the area.

Healing miracles opened doors for the preaching of the gospel. Some who insist that healing was only given for the apostolic age point to the fact of healings opening doors to the gospel, arguing that healing miracles were only intended to authenticate the deity of Christ and the validity of the Gospel, and that there was no more need for miracles after that time. But the gospel still has not reached the whole world; therefore, there is still need for the manifestation of the supernatural to open doors.

However, on the other hand, a close study of healings will show that many had no relationship to "opening doors," being simply a manifestation of the mercy and compassion of the Lord. In a number of the healing miracles of Jesus, the text states that He was "moved with compassion." Let us be certain: Jesus did not cut off the flow of His mercy and compassion with the end of the apostolic age. In fact, the Bible does not even mention an "apostolic age." When Jesus said, "These signs will follow those who believe," He did not add, "until the apostles die." As long as there are preachers who believe the Word and believe that Jesus is the same, there will be miracles of healing: some who need to open doors, some who share in Christ's compassion, and some who obey the apostolic admonition of James to lay hands on the sick.

Take time to reflect on "compassion as a motive for healing ministry." "Power," "excitement," and "evangelism" are often preoccupying ideas around signs and wonders, but the ministry of compassion needs to be thoughtfully considered. What do you think? Write your response.

Healing at Joppa (Acts 9:36–43)

When Peter had ministered in Lydda with the result that the whole community accepted Christ, He was called from Joppa to pray for a lovely lady who had died. Her name, Dorcas, meant "Gazelle." She probably received that name because it was noticed that she was very active, yet delicate. Dorcas, whose equivalent Hebrew name was Tabitha, labored endlessly, making garments for the widows of her area. She was naturally loved by all the people. When she died, perhaps from excessive work, the whole community mourned. Having heard of the healing miracle in Lydda at the hands of Peter, they implored him to come to Joppa to pray for Dorcas.

Peter responded to the summons. When he arrived, he found the house full of widows mourning the loss of their benefactor. Dorcas loved people; they reciprocated that love. Peter cleared the room, prayed the prayer of faith, said, "Tabitha, arise," and took her by the hand, lifting her up, and presented her alive. What a wonderful gift to the widows of Joppa! As a result of the healing miracle—actually a restoration of life—many in Joppa joined their neighbors in Lydda and Sharon as devout Christian believers.

Peter's stay in Joppa put him in the position to respond to the call he would get from Cornelius, the Roman centurion in whose house Peter would lead the first fully Gentile group to the knowledge of Jesus the Savior. What happened there fulfilled the prophecy of Jesus concerning the projection of the gospel message.

What do the following Scripture passages have in common with Acts 9:36–43?

Luke 7:11–17

Luke 8:48–56

John 11:38–44

HEALING IN THE MINISTRY OF PAUL

While Peter was ministering in the area nearer to the Roman Caesarea, Saul of Tarsus was being miraculously converted to Christ. Divine providence was shaping an instrument that would reap the whitened fields of the Roman Empire. After his conversion (Acts 9:1–31), his spiritual retreat to Arabia, and his receiving of the right hand of fellowship from the church leaders, Saul joined Barnabas in Antioch from which missionary base he would carry the gospel to Rome and beyond (Acts 11:19–30; 12:25—13:3).

Healing at Cyprus

First Paul and Barnabas ministered in Cyprus where they had a reverse miracle, if such there is. A sorcerer named Elymas was endeavoring to corrupt the mind of the Proconsul Sergius Paulus. Paul, led of the Spirit, rebuked the spiritist who, as a result, was stricken blind. The proconsul, seeing the divine judgment upon an agent of Satan, embraced the Lord wholeheartedly. Read Acts 13:4–12. What most impresses you as you read of this power-work?

Healings at Iconium

Paul and Barnabas next preached the gospel in Antioch of Pisidia and Iconium (Acts 13:13—14:6). They stayed for a long time in Iconium where God gave them "wonders" to arouse their interests, and "signs" to demonstrate to them the mercy and goodness of the Lord. They were able to win many souls among both the Jews and the Gentiles. However, persecution by both Jews and unbelieving city leaders forced the apostles to flee to Lystra to escape stoning. Read Acts 14:1–7. In the light of verse 3, "bearing witness to the word of His grace," write your thoughts comparing the grace of God that heals us with the grace that saves us from sin.

Healing at Lystra

Paul's first recorded identifiable miracle took place in Lystra. Read Acts 14:8–20.

What was the condition healed?

What prompted Paul's summons to health?

What motivated the man's faith?

What was the crowd's reaction; then, what was the apostle's response?

What two things conclude the account?

The man healed in Lystra, again, was a paralytic, a cripple who had never walked. A miracle was needed in Lystra to open the door to the gospel. Again the healing was of a visible type upon a man, well known in the city. When Paul saw the man, God gave to the apostle the witness that the cripple had faith to believe. At once Paul commanded the man with the words, "Stand up straight on your feet!" When the cripple jumped to his feet for the first time, the witnessing crowd went wild. The pagan people of Lystra assumed that Paul and Barnabas were gods come down to earth, Zeus and Hermes (in Roman mythology, Jupiter and Mercury), and they started to worship them and to sacrifice to them. Only with difficulty did they restrain them. In spite of the miracle, the Jews and other opponents of the faith stoned Paul and left him for dead. (The Christian groups in Antioch of Pisidia, Iconium, Lystra, and Derbe are the churches Paul wrote to as the Galatian churches. Their vacillation is spelled out in the Galatian letter.)

Healing at Philippi

Paul's next healing miracle happened in Europe, in Philippi. In fact, Paul's liberation of a girl fortune-teller, whom unscrupulous men were exploiting for financial gain, landed him and Silas in the Philippian jail. Read Acts 16:16–34.

Describe Paul's early and later responses to the demonized girl.

What do you conclude from her shoutings—that is, the demon's objective?

What five key events proceed upon her deliverance?

Paul suffered the girl's divination of his ministry for some days. Satan was using the girl to discredit Paul by making people think that the apostle was associated in some way with the divination scheme. If Satan cannot defeat us, he will try to stamp us with his insignia. The defeated exploiters got the apostles in jail, but God broke them out; and a precious family was won to Christ. Imprisonment behind bars might have discouraged some people, but Paul and Silas sang the bars open. The world can never defeat you if it can't quiet your song (Eph. 5:18, 19).

Healings at Ephesus
Paul's greatest healing ministry was exercised in Ephesus:

Now God worked unusual miracles by the hands of Paul, so that even handkerchiefs or aprons were brought from his body to the sick, and the diseases left them and the evil spirits went out of them.
(Acts 19:11, 12)

From this passage comes the occasional practice today of sending anointed handkerchiefs to the sick. There is no healing power in the handkerchief; it is simply an aid to faith, a point of contact. The anointed cloth may abet the faith both of the sender and the receiver; faith from the elder who anoints the cloth may also be added. It is a matter of two or three agreeing together in the name of Jesus. Faith in agreement God honors.

Not only were the sick and afflicted healed under Paul's Ephesian ministry, but demon spirits were cast out. Ephesus was a center of pagan worship—not only the worship of Diana, but every form of occult practice. Multitudes who had given Satan access through these spiritist seances were possessed or oppressed by evil spirits. Exorcism of demon spirits was a part of Paul's wide ministry.

Reading Acts 19:1–28, noting especially (a) verses 17–20, then (b) verses 23–28, how would you assess Paul's ministry in Ephesus and the general response of the multitudes? Compare your observations as to the masses' response to gospel power today.

Here in Ephesus, the greater part of Paul's healing ministry is described in the term "unusual miracles." They were unusual in their effect and unusual in their number. Paul's Ephesian ministry was his most successful and longest lasting. During those more than two years, the gospel reached most of the area known then as Asia (Acts 19:10). So large was the Christian community in Ephesus that scores of Christian homes had to be used for worship and as meeting places.

Using a concordance, how many scripture passages can you find which refer to the exorcism of demon spirits?

What help do you find in Ephesians 6:10–20 for the defeat of Satanic powers?

Healings in Malta

At Caesarea, Paul, a Roman citizen, appealed to Caesar to escape from the fury of the Jews. Before King Agrippa he had recounted his miraculous conversion and the revealed purpose of God for his life (Acts 26:15–19).

Before Paul's writing an epistle to the Romans, he had felt a strong conviction that he would minister in Rome (Rom. 1:15). In Acts 19:21 he said, "I must also see Rome." While Paul was still in Jerusalem, detained by the Jewish council, God had spoken to Paul these words: "Be of good cheer, Paul; for as you have testified for Me in Jerusalem, so also you must also bear witness at Rome" (Acts 23:11). Chapters 27 and 28 of Acts describe Paul's journey by ship to Rome. The apostle had suffered shipwreck before (see 2 Cor. 11:25), but his most devastating storm and shipwreck he experienced on the journey to Rome. He and others survived and came ashore at the Island of Malta. "And the natives showed us unusual kindness;

for they kindled a fire and made us all welcome, because of the rain that was falling and because of the cold" (Acts 28:2). The word "natives" in the Greek is "barbarous." The Greeks called all peoples barbarian who did not speak Greek or Latin. Actually, the Maltese were a civilized people of Phoenician origin; however, they had never heard the gospel. They were a benevolent people, for the word translated "kindness" is in Greek "philanthropian." We call anyone who gives large sums of money to charity a "philanthropist," which means "one who loves mankind." The people of Malta gave Paul and the shipwrecked passengers a loving welcome.

Read Acts 28:1–10 and record the miracle that amazed the people and the healing Paul ministered to Publius.

When Paul shook off the snake into the fire, and after some time showed no ill effects, they took him for a god. The serpent experience fulfilled what Scripture had prophesied in Mark's form of the great commission (Mark 16:18): "<u>They will take up serpents</u>; and if they drink anything deadly, it will by no means hurt them; <u>they will lay hands on the sick, and they will recover</u>."

 KINGDOM EXTRA

Paul's Healing Ministry in Malta. In Acts 28:8, 9 is a reference to divine healings in spite of the fact that Luke, a physician, accompanied Paul. This fact is so troublesome to critics of modern healing that some have come forth with the theory that the healings mentioned in verse 9 were the work of Luke who used medical remedies, although Luke is not mentioned by name. The theory is based on the use of *therapeuo,* the Greek word for "healing" (v. 8) which some insist refers to medical therapy.

In fact, however, this word occurs thirty-four times in the New Testament. In thirty-two instances it clearly refers to divine healing; in the other cases the use is general. Both words *iaomai* and *therapeuo* are used in reference to the same healing in Matthew 8:7, 8 indicating that the terms are used interchangeably in the Bible. This observation is certainly not to oppose medical treatment or to say that medicine or medical aid is wrong. It is not. However, it does clarify that this text is not grounds for the substitution of medical therapy for prayer. God heals by many means: the prayer of faith, natural recuperative powers, medical aid or medicine, miracles.[3]

Paul's shipwreck at Malta, while a painful experience in the flesh, became, in God's providence, an opportunity to bring the gospel to a previously unevangelized people. Nowhere does it mention that Paul or any of his party preached the gospel at Malta, but as G. Campbell Morgan states in his commentary on Acts, the evangelization was accomplished through the healing ministry. As people were prayed for in Malta in the name of Jesus, it was explained to them that Jesus was the Savior of the world, the Healer of spirit, soul, mind, and body. In Jesus one finds wholeness. From Paul's day on, Malta was a Christianized island. As we well know, Paul arrived in Rome, revived the Roman church, and gave his life as a martyr. From Rome he wrote several of his epistles; through them and in Christ, he has blessed the world.

Much that we know about divine healing, we have learned by the examples of healings from the apostolic ministries of Peter, Stephen, Philip, and Paul as recorded in Acts. Not a word do we find in the Acts of the Apostles of any suggestion that healing ministries were coming to an end. The church of Jesus Christ goes on, and every blessing of Christ's atoning death on the Cross will continue until He comes back again. May God help us all to live in the faith that the blessed Holy Spirit supplies!

1. *Spirit-Filled Life Bible* (Nashville, TN: Thomas Nelson Publishers, 1991), 1502, "Word Wealth: 16:20 confirming."
2. Ibid., 1501–1502, note on 16:9–20.
3. Ibid., 1681, "Kingdom Dynamics: Paul's Healing Ministry in Malta."

Lesson 12/An Optimum Climate for Healing

Genuine faith in God is not merely believing something about God, although it begins with belief that God is able. Effective faith believes that God is a covenant-making and keeping God; and it takes a step mentally or physically in the direction of God's covenant promise.

- Noah prepared an ark.
- Abraham went out not knowing where he was going.
- Isaac blessed Jacob . . . concerning things to come.
- Moses forsook Egypt not fearing the wrath of the king; by faith they passed through the Red Sea as by dry land, and so on.

All of God's men and women of faith took a step before seeing the fulfillment of God's covenant promise.

For a scripture passage that provides help in tracing the steps toward the cultivation of faith, read Mark 9:17–29.

 KINGDOM EXTRA

Cultivating a Climate of Faith for Healing. In [Mark 9:17–29] Jesus tells us that "believing" is the condition for answered prayer for a healing. The father of the demon-possessed boy answered in tears, "I believe," then added "help my unbelief!" Since faith is a gift, we may pray for it as this father did. Note how quickly God's grace answered; but there is another lesson. Where an atmosphere of unbelief makes it difficult to believe, we should seek a different setting. Even Jesus' ability to work miracles was reduced where unbelief prevailed (Matt. 13:58).

Prayer and praise provide an atmosphere of faith in God. In this text Jesus explained another obstacle to faith's victory—why their prayers had been fruitless: "This kind can come out by nothing but prayer and fasting" (Mark 9:29). His explanation teaches: 1) some (not all) affliction is demonically imposed; and 2) some kinds of demonic bondage do not respond to exorcism, but only to fervent prayer. Continuance in prayer, accompanied by praise, and sometimes fasting, provides a climate for faith that brings deliverance.[1]

Our leading scripture text is preceded in Mark's gospel by the account of the transfiguration of Jesus our Lord. He took with Him the three disciples who were closest in fellowship to Him. They met there with Moses and Elijah who discussed with Him His death and resurrection, and the full significance of His atoning work (Luke 9:30, 31). There a union of the Redeemer and the representatives of the Law and the Prophets took place. New Testament apostles and Old Testament prophets met with the glorified Christ in the center (Mark 9:1-13; Matt. 17:1-13; Luke 9:27-36; John 12:23-28). There was a preview of the incomparable event that would make available to believers of all time the full power of redemption.

In the valley below, a quarreling multitude with an afflicted boy in the center anxiously waited for Jesus, Peter, James, and John to return and help. The disciples left behind at the foot of the mountain were disputing with the unbelieving scribes (Mark 9:14) over the power of the disciples to heal the demon-possessed boy. They had exorcised the demon, but with no success. The father met Jesus with the heartrending cry, "Your disciples could do nothing; if You can do anything, have compassion and help us."

The climate for healing was impossible:

1. It was a climate of strife and argument, not one of harmony and peace;

2. It was a climate of unbelief; the scribes and their sympathizers were denying the lordship of Jesus, often accusing Him of casting out demons by Beelzebub;
3. The strife and unbelief created a climate of doubt and bewilderment on the part of the father;
4. The failure of the disciples had undermined their confidence in the gift Jesus had previously given them;
5. The general multitude were running around in amazement, with everyone expressing some point of view regarding the matter at hand.

Before proceeding, think through each of the five points above. How do these manifest today?

Now, let us contrast our analysis with a look at the kind of climate needed to create an atmosphere for complete, God-glorifying healing to take place.

1. A CLIMATE OF POSITIVE FAITH

Even Jesus did not perform many miracles where there was a climate of unbelief (Matt. 13:57, 58). If even Jesus, the Great Physician, was to some degree restrained in His working of healing miracles, we should not be surprised that the modern healings result, more often than not, in an atmosphere of faith and assurance, such as a congregation of believers, a circle of elders—several holding hands and praying—and a number of persons in agreement after an anointed sermon, after several healing testimonies, in an atmosphere of praise and worship.

In the account of the healing of the demon-possessed boy, Jesus explained the failure of the disciples to effect his healing as follows in Matthew 17:20: "Because of your unbelief; for assuredly, I say to you, if you have faith as a mustard seed, you will say to this mountain, 'Move from here to there,' and it will move; and nothing will be impossible for you."

From the following scripture passages, explain how faith is manifested in the result.

Matt. 9:27–30

Matt. 15:21–28

Matt. 21:18–22

Mark 5:27–34

2. A CLIMATE OF HARMONY AND AGREEMENT

Jesus made the following promise to His disciples: "Again I say to you that if two of you agree on earth concerning anything that they ask, it will be done for them by My Father in heaven. For where two or three are gathered together in My name, I am there in the midst of them" (Matt. 18:19, 20).

When Jesus and the three disciples came down from the Mount of Transfiguration, they came with heavenly glory for earth's dreary afflictions. When they joined the waiting disciples they entered an atmosphere of theological conflict and doubt born of failure. Believers debated with unbelievers. Attempts were made to lift the awful burden of demon possession with no success. The very presence of Jesus, the Lord of Glory, the Prince of Peace, transformed the climate from debate to expectancy, from doubt to hope, from despair to confidence. Where the presence of Jesus is, dead hopes are resurrected.

Church members need to constantly remind themselves of the importance of the presence of the Lord in every church service. We should enter the sanctuary in a spirit of expectancy, leaving behind every spirit or attitude of doubt, conflict, frivolity, or skepticism. It is so important to create in the house of God a climate for healing of body, soul, mind, and spirit. The more there is agreement, the more there is healing from the clear presence of Jesus.

WORD WEALTH

With one accord, *homothumadon.* Being unanimous, having mutual consent, being in agreement, having group unity, having one mind and purpose. The disciples had an intellectual unanimity, an emotional rapport, and volitional agreement in the newly founded church. In each of its occurrences, *homothumadon* shows a harmony leading to action.[2]

Examine the following passages and note the common denominator that is expressed in certain words. What are they? Also, in each situation, record the results of such a climate.

Acts 1:14

Acts 2:1

Acts 2:46

Acts 4:24

Acts 5:12

Acts 8:6

3. A CLIMATE OF HUMILITY

It appears that the disciples were guilty of more than conflict with the scribes. In Mark 9:33–37, another hindrance to
faith was brought to light—lack of humility.

 KINGDOM EXTRA

Childlikeness. Jesus confronts the tendency of
humankind to associate authority with an exercise of domi-
nance over others. The dominion or authority in kingdom life
God wants to reinstate in us is for victorious, fruitful living and
for the overthrow of hellish powers, not for gaining control of
others or for serving our own interests. His call to childlike
humility and a servantlike heart (John 13:1–17) establishes
the spirit and style by which the authority of the believer is to
be exercised as an agent of God's kingdom power. (See Matt.
19:14; Mark 10:14, 15; Luke 18:16, 17.)[3]

It seems likely that the apostles who remained behind during the Transfiguration spent some time discussing their
respective places in Christ's coming kingdom—who would
occupy first place, who would receive highest honors, who
would be carved the highest on the totem pole? Jesus was fully
aware of their thoughts and reasonings, as He is aware of the
selfish ambitions of all of us. Jesus set a little child in the center
of the circle, declaring, "This is My model to be emulated; if
you want to be a ruler, become a servant. All the big people in
the kingdom of God will have come out of servanthood."

Read Philippians 2:1–5. List the attributes and acts of
humility called for.

4. A Climate of Concern and Guidance

It seems very clear that Jesus had a wider interest in the case than of the miracle alone. Obviously, the father needed guidance and assurance almost as much as the boy needed healing. The Lord posed the question, "How long has this been happening to him?" There is no doubt that the conversation between Jesus and the boy's father was much more extended than that which is reported. That which is reported definitely shows that Jesus was diagnosing and treating the anxiety and frustration of the demoniac's father. To Jesus, the healing of the father was essential to the healing of the son. There are times when the spiritual healing of a whole family is the prelude to the physical healing of the sick one.

When Jesus healed the daughter of Jairus (Mark 5:35–43), He cleared the room of curious neighbors and took with Him into the room where the deceased child lay only the parents and the believing disciples. When He said, *Talitha, cumi,* "Little girl, arise," He was speaking in household Aramaic; the words He uttered were for the sake of the family who needed spiritual healing. Sometimes in order for a sick person to be healed, there must be a healing of the whole environment, a transformation of the climate.

Can you think of situations where people often ask for prayer for healing and what is more needed is wise counsel and practical behavioral change? Give examples that come to mind.

5. A Climate of Dependence

The demoniac boy's father was understandably discouraged; his response to Jesus was, "If You can do anything, have compassion on us and help us." If he had doubts about the omnipotence of Jesus, he retained some belief in His compassion. As we have seen, some teachers, believing that miracles were performed only to establish the deity of Christ, contend that Jesus concluded His bodily healing provision with the end of a supposed apostolic age.

We believe that it can be established that Jesus healed in a great number of instances because of His compassion. If Jesus *ever* healed at all out of compassion, He must still have that same compassion, for He is forever the same (Heb. 13:8). If Jesus healed only as a credential of His deity, then the Bible authors were mistaken as to His motivation. The boy's father appealed to the compassion of Jesus. Jesus answered the father, in effect, "If I can do anything? I truly came out of love to redeem people from the kingdom of Satan, but the condition for all of My salvation blessing is 'faith.' By works, no one could merit divine healing of body and soul, but if you can 'believe,' all things are possible."

The boy's father responded, "Lord, I believe"! He had believed enough to bring his diabolically afflicted boy to Jesus, but the disciples' inability to exorcise the demon had filled his heart with doubt. Which of us would have reacted differently? However, the father demonstrated his trusting spirit by calling from the depth of his anguished soul, "Help my unbelief!"

Pause to write ways and situations where you long for an increase of faith. Write a prayer, expressing it all.

There are several ways to increase our faith: 1) "faith comes by hearing, and hearing by the word of God"; 2) faith comes from prayer, from making the increasing of our faith the subject of our petitions; 3) faith increases from the exercise of it; the more we trust God as our Helper in everything we do, the more faith we have for the big challenges. Utter corporate dependence upon the Lord is the finest way to create a climate for healing.

6. A CLIMATE OF PRAYER AND PRAISE

After Jesus had delivered the demoniac boy, His disciples approached Him with the anxious question, "Why could we not cast it out?" They had exorcised demon spirits before. A number of answers could have been given, some of which we have suggested, but it happened that this boy's particular type of demon possession required a kind of curative of which they had not previously been aware. The boy's kind of satanic bondage could not be overcome by simple exorcism. Jesus, who came to destroy the works of the Devil, casts out the demon, then says His servants could deliver that kind of bondage only by prayer and fasting.

There is some question about the word *fasting*. It is not found in some earlier manuscripts, but the text of the New King James Version follows the Majority text which retains the word *fasting*. The general idea here, however, is that the boy's kind of bondage could only be healed by supernaturally empowered praying.

In connection with the New Testament healing covenant, James said, "The effective, fervent prayer of a righteous man avails much." Usually it takes time and holy concentration in prayer to energize it in the anointing of the Holy Spirit.

 KINGDOM EXTRA

Effectivity in Spiritual Warfare. James pictures a level of prayer that is beyond a believer's normal capacity—it is divinely energized by the direct involvement of the Holy Spirit. The Greek word for "fervent" actually does not appear in the original text. It is an amplification of the word for "effectual" which does appear in the Greek text. The Greek word *energeo* means "effectual, or that which is made effective." Yet, to simply say prayer is "effective when offered by a righteous person" was deemed by the translators to be shallow in the context, and therefore "fervent" was rightly added to the text. To fully understand the word *energeo* one needs to examine another passage where the word is used. Paul used the word in describing the power of God's Word as it works special energy in those who believe (1 Thess. 2:13). The foundational promise of the Greek word *energeo* is that something "effectively works." Yet it only works in those who "believe." Applied to this text, this suggests that our praying, when energized by the power of the Holy Spirit, causes things to happen. Our prayers work![4]

Spiritual warfare through prayer is much needed against the powers of darkness. Paul wrote to the Colossian believers, speaking of his prayers for them: "To this *end* I also labor, striving according to His working which works in me mightily. For I want you to know what a great conflict I have for you and those in Laodicea, and *for* as many as have not seen my face in the flesh" (Col. 1:29—2:1). Paul uses terms, such as *labor, striving,* and *conflict,* to describe his manner of spiritual warfare in their behalf. There can be no finer climate for healing and deliverance than that of intensive, corporate prayer.

In recent times there has been a new awakening in the church to the need for intensive prayer, a spiritual warfare against all those forces which hinder the church's work to rescue the lost and to bring total healing to those who will receive it. The church is responding anew to the challenge of the apostle Paul (see Eph. 6:10–12).

In Colossians 4:12, Paul identifies again the area of our warfare: "Epaphras, who is *one* of you, a bondservant of Christ, greets you, always <u>laboring</u> <u>fervently</u> for you <u>in</u> <u>prayers,</u> that you may stand perfect and complete in all the will of God." The words "laboring fervently" translate the Greek word *agonizomai,* which is usually translated "fight," "striving," "conflict," "struggle." It is a word definitely related to "warfare." Paul used the same word when he said, "I have fought a good fight." He employs it in another passage (1 Tim. 6:12) where he admonishes, "Fight the good fight of faith." Since the believer's battle is against unseen evil forces, his only truly effective weapon is prayer, intensive prayer anointed by the Spirit.

In Romans 15:30, 31, we have a scripture passage that vividly illustrates the importance of prayer in spiritual warfare: "Now I beg you, brethren, through the Lord Jesus Christ, and through the love of the Spirit, that you strive together with me in prayers to God for me, that I may be delivered from those in Judea who do not believe, and that my service for Jerusalem may be acceptable to the saints." Paul planned to visit Rome, but he wanted first to visit Jerusalem. He was well aware of the opposition to him that he would find in Jerusalem, but he had an offering for the poor saints and he wanted to carry out the project; he hoped that the gesture of love from the Gentile churches would heal the animosity toward his ministry. He knew that only intensive prayer could heal the wound. The prayers were answered, but not in the way he expected. He escaped from the enemies and he made it to Rome, but only after arrests, trials, and a journey to Rome in irons interrupted by shipwreck. Yet out of it all we have the books of Ephesians, Philippians, Colossians, Philemon, and 2 Timothy. On his journey to Rome he evangelized the island of Malta. In Rome as a prisoner, he wrote to the Philippians, reporting that "the things which *happened* to me have actually turned out for the furtherance of the gospel" (Phil. 1:12).

 FAITH ALIVE

In this chapter we have endeavored to pinpoint the values that enhance the climate for healing. These values we have discovered in the account of the healing of the demon-possessed boy whom Jesus delivered on the occasion of His descent from the Mount of Transfiguration. That the Lord intended the story to be a pattern for us to interpret is suggested by its occurrence in three of the four Gospels. In the account, a number of circumstances appeared to hinder or make more difficult the miracle of deliverance. The obstacles to healing seemed to be the following: strife, self-seeking, discouragement, and unbelief. The values that brought healing were agreement, humility, faith, perseverance, prayer, and spiritual warfare.

Having concluded, review the major points in this chapter and consider how you may apply its principles to impact the "climate" of your own faith life.

1. *Spirit-Filled Life Bible* (Nashville, TN: Thomas Nelson Publishers, 1991), 1486, "Kingdom Dynamics: Cultivating a Climate of Faith for Healing."
2. Ibid., 1624, "Word Wealth: 2:1 with one accord."
3. Ibid., 1439, "Kingdom Dynamics: Childlikeness."
4. Ibid., 1902, "Kingdom Dynamics: Effectivity in Spiritual Warfare."

Lesson 13/Divine Healing— Answering the Doubters

Sound theology is simply right Bible teaching. Is the doctrine of divine healing by the power of the Holy Spirit correct doctrine? Of course, many do not believe the Bible. And not everyone who believes the Bible in general believes in divine healing or the miraculous specifically. Not everyone who believes in the miracles of Jesus' time believes that miracles— especially healing miracles—can or should be expected today.

The position of this study guide is that Christ's redeeming work on the Cross, which was culminated at His resurrection and ascension, was effective for the whole person for the entire church age. In this chapter we will endeavor to give an answer to the objections to divine healing.

1. Possibly the most common objection to divine healing is that it is not scientific. [By "divine healing" we mean "the power of God to heal or deliver the sick and afflicted through Bible-believing prayer in the name of Jesus Christ of Nazareth."] Those who hold this view object to any kind of miracle. "The day of miracles is past," is commonly claimed. These define "miracle" as something contrary to the laws of nature. The problem with that definition is that the more we come to know, the more we discover that nature is beyond our comprehension. Only "mathematics" approaches being an exact science; so-called laws are simply "probabilities." If we accept the existence of an intelligent Supreme Being who created the universe, we must conclude that He can intervene in His creation.

Naturalism

There are some, called naturalists, who, if they hold any belief in a God, believe He created the universe, but has left it to run by itself by fixed laws. In short, there is no "personal" God attentive to us in our personal concerns. But if there is an intelligent Supreme Being who created humankind, it is unthinkable that He would do so without somewhere revealing to His creatures His will and purpose for them. Though some think that He revealed Himself only in nature itself, nature does not tell us from where we came, where we are going, why we are here, or how our Creator can be approached. Humankind yearns to know the answer to these important questions. If God exists at all, it is far more believable than not that He must have created us to know Him and to commune with Him.

Atheism

Of course, a popular theory of our day is that which denies the existence of the God of the Bible and theorizes that the universe has always existed and that man evolved from a spark of life that happened by chance. First of all, there are three possibilities for the universe:

1. It always existed. But this is impossible since the Second Law of Thermodynamics reveals that the whole universe is losing energy and, since this is so, there has to be a time when it began.
2. The universe just happened from nothing, by itself. But an ancient and accepted rule of logic is that "from nothing, nothing comes."
3. The universe was created by an omnipotent, all-wise God, a belief that man everywhere has originally accepted and which a majority of humankind still believes.

That human life could come from a simple virus, or amoeba, springing from inert matter by spontaneous generation, is unthinkable. In his work, *Origins of Life* (Lion Publishing, 1985), scientist Jim Brooks addresses the possibility of life happening by chance pointing out that not even a simple protein could happen by chance.

If it is true
* that the universe has not always existed, and
* that it could not have emerged from nothing,
then it must have been created by an all-powerful, all-wise Creator.

If an intelligent God created everything, including the human race—for which He has provided a plan of redemption, we may be certain that He who intervened by supernatural means to rescue us may intervene in any way and at any time that is within the scope of His purpose. He who supernaturally intervened in human affairs for thousands of years may continue to work among us as it fits into His program of redemption. He who healed multitudes of sick people, as recorded on the pages of the New Testament, would not have withdrawn His mercies without notice. And He's never given such notice! It is entirely and scientifically credible to believe He heals and that He heals today!

2. A second objection to contemporary biblical healing ministry is that God gave miracles in the first age to confirm the truth and validity of Christianity, and now that Christianity is established, there is no longer a need for divine healing as a means of confirming the gospel truths. This argument fails on its own proposition, for most who propose it believe in supernatural conversion. And if this were God's purpose that miracles cease, there would be no more need either for supernatural conversion and regeneration. The transformation of a life is an even greater miracle than a healing. So why diminish or remove the place of the lesser as either unworthy or unavailable?

Furthermore, it can be shown that many of the miracles were attributed to the compassion of Jesus, not to confirm His authority; in fact, many times Jesus admonished the healed persons to keep silent about the miracle. The following passages contain statements of the compassion of Jesus as His motive for healing the sick: Matthew 9:35, 36; 14:14; 20:33, 34; Mark 5:19, 20; 9:22; and Luke 7:13, 14. There are also at least five passages where Jesus responded, with healing, to those who appealed to Him with the words, "Have mercy" (Matt. 9:27; 15:22–28; 17:15; 20:30; Luke 18:38, 39).

3. A third objection to present-day healing is that Jesus healed the sick in His day because physical medicine had not progressed to the state of development that made it reliable, and since today medical science has been perfected, supernatural healing is no longer needed.

First, this objection misses the point. Divine healing is not a physical blessing only; it is an even greater spiritual blessing. Our bodies are temples of the Holy Spirit which have been redeemed by the atoning work of Christ; since we are bought with a price, we are to glorify the Lord in our bodies as well as in our spirits. Paul admonished, "Present your bodies a living sacrifice." The health of the soul and spirit affect the physical body; and a divinely healthy body strengthens the mind and spirit.

As to the development of medical science, it should be pointed out that Hippocrates, the father of scientific medicine, lived four hundred years before Christ. Luke, who wrote the gospel of his name and the Book of Acts, was a physician whose competence is evidenced by his use of medical terms and understanding of diseases, yet there is no suggestion that he assisted Paul in the healing of the sick except as one agreeing in prayer. If divine healing was destined to cease with the death of the apostles, there should have been a great breakthrough in medical science at the end of the first century, but such is not the case; medical science did not improve appreciably until the Renaissance period, and, in reality, not until the more recent discovery of antibiotics. Further, health care and insurance costs today have become so expensive that many cannot afford it, thus increasing the need for divine healing.

It must be said here that God has given mankind many substances with healing value. He has gifted many dedicated persons with healing cures that are an indescribable blessing to humanity. Many Christian organizations have built and maintain hospitals for the care of the sick and afflicted. All of this certainly can be considered a blessing from God. The work of doctors and surgeons can be made even more skillful with the unseen hand of the Great Physician. Christians should be able to resort to available curative science without any sense of guilt; but the blessing of divine healing by the power of the Holy Spirit, in answer to the prayer of faith, is truly a sacrament of the church and a special provision for believers. It is a precious expectation of the children of the Lord. The relative state of the medical arts really has nothing to do with the validity, the need, or the place, of divine healing in the church.

4. A fourth objection to modern divine healing is that divine healing ceased after the apostolic age. This claim is not true. History records a number of reliable testimonies to divine healing in answer to prayer. The following are men of God who reported healings in their day:

1. Justin Martyr in A.D. 165, sixty-five years after the close of the apostolic age.
2. Irenaeus in A.D. 192 mentions gifts of healing and the laying on of hands to heal the sick.
3. Tertullian in A.D. 216 mentions healings of people of all ages and stations of life. These healings included expulsion of demons.
4. Origen in A.D. 250 mentions healings of many kinds of diseases. A number had gifts of healings.
5. Clement of Alexandria in A.D. 275 mentions the gifts of healings, and prayer with fasting for healing.
6. Theodore of Mopsueste in A.D. 429 (more than three hundred years after the end of the first century) reports an abundance of healings, including healings of the heathen.
7. Gregory the Great, A.D. 500—when a missionary to Briton—prayed for the sick, anointing them with oil.
   John Wesley attributes the decline in miracles of healing after Gregory until the Protestant Reformation to a spiritual decline. With the Reformation came a new spiritual awakening.
8. The Waldenses, a devoutly spiritual group of the twelfth century, in their Confession of Faith, express strong faith in divine healing in answer to prayer.
9. Count Zinzendorf, A.D. 1725, of the Moravian movement (United Brethren), reports a number of healing miracles in answer to prayer.
10. John Wesley, A.D. 1750, graduate of Oxford University and founder of the Methodist Church, makes a number of entries in his diary of healings.

Both the Bible and history are in agreement that divine healing is an integral part of the ministry of the church.

5. A fifth objection to divine healing as a ministry of the modern church is that if we accept healing, must we not also raise the dead, speak in other tongues, take up serpents, and drink poisons without harm?

Divine healing is a part of Christ's atoning work along with pardon for transgressions as prophesied by Isaiah and confirmed by Matthew (Matt. 8). The Great Commission of Mark 16 does not mention the raising of the dead, nor do any of the healing covenants. There have been cases of the dead being raised during church history, but they are instances of miracles, not of abiding blessings promised to us. God in His great mercy does many things as a sovereign Lord, but we haven't a "covenant right" to claim the release of one from death in the same way we have been given the covenant of healing.

As regarding the speaking with tongues, it is both a gift and a prayer blessing for believers. Some respond with the verse in 1 Corinthians 13, "Tongues shall cease" (1 Cor. 13:8). But they overlook the clause that tells *when* tongues, prophecy, and knowledge will be done away, which is, "When that which is perfect is come, then that which is in part shall be done away" (1 Cor. 13:10). That which is perfect will not come until Jesus returns in glory.

Mark's Great Commission does predict that those who believe will take up serpents and drink poisons without harm; however, these promises have to do with unavoidable instances of these perils. It was never intended that believers would deliberately handle snakes or drink poisons to demonstrate the power of God; in fact, to do so would be the sin of tempting God. A number of missionaries have testified to being protected from these perils, just as we have seen Paul was on the Island of Malta (Acts 28).

6. A sixth objection to the doctrine of divine healing is that if all sick people would always be healed, no one would ever die. This, of course, is not taught by the Bible nor by any orthodox teachers of the divine healing doctrine. The Bible

tells us plainly that "it is appointed for men to die once" (Heb. 9:27). All of the apostles died, some of them at a rather early age. God has given promises of protection, provision, healing, and many others; but, of course, all promises are subject to higher purposes of a sovereign God.

Paul gives us a good example of the working of providence in the first chapter of Philippians (Phil. 1:20–26).

Paul was aware of the fact that, being under arrest, he could be put to death at any time. But, his earnest desire was simply that whether by life or death, Christ might be magnified in his body. To him to die would have been gain, but to live would have been continued service to his beloved Master. He finally came to the conviction that he would remain in body longer to minister to the churches.

Paul's will was subservient to God's will. He was fully in subjection to God's plan for his ministry and earthly life. God's promises are yea and amen, but the promises are subject to His overall providence.

We know that God's general will for all His children is spiritual and physical health. We do not always discern where our life's circumstances fit into His sovereign plan, but in practical experience we stand on His promises in His Word. We do not always know just how to pray, but in that case His Spirit prays through us in His prayer language (Rom. 8:26, 27).

7. A seventh objection to the healing doctrine is that there are examples of failure in the New Testament—Christian workers who were sick. The Bible, of course, does not say that a believer will never be sick, but it does say that the prayer of faith will save the sick. Healing is conditional on obedience, faith, and the providential moment.

Persons who advance this objection usually point to Paul's thorn in the flesh (2 Cor. 12:7); Trophimus's being left sick (2 Tim. 4:20); Timothy's drinking wine for his stomach's sake (1 Tim. 5:23); and Epaphroditus, the pastor of the church at Philippi (Phil. 2:25–27).

Regarding Paul's thorn, we do not know what it was. If God had intended for us to know, it would have been identified. If we did know, all kinds of people would be claiming Paul's thorn. There was a clear, providential reason for the thorn that was given to Paul to keep him humble in view of his abundance of revelations. (Unless one has had several visits to the third heaven, perhaps one should not expect a counterbalancing thorn!)

When we consider that Paul was constantly ministering, along with earning his living by tentmaking, that in his many travels he was stoned, shipwrecked several times, and imprisoned several times, we must conclude that his health was quite robust. In 2 Corinthians 11 he gives a whole list of his labors, tribulations, and persecutions, but makes no reference whatever to sickness.

The reference to the sickness of Trophimus is so brief that we know nothing of the circumstances. Many healings are not immediate. We know nothing of the faith or spiritual state of Trophimus. Furthermore, we do not base a doctrine on people or their circumstances, we base our convictions upon the Word of God and its promises.

Paul's advice to Timothy to take wine for his stomach's sake was neither a medical suggestion nor a boost for wine drinking; it was a caution against drinking the polluted water in Timothy's location.

Epaphroditus's case is a plus for divine healing, for we are told that God healed him (Phil. 2:25–28). Epaphroditus became ill from the strenuous journey he made from Philippi to Rome to deliver an offering and news to the imprisoned apostle. Paul's mention of sorrow upon sorrow means that if Epaphroditus, his young friend, had died, it would have been a sorrowful loss of a treasured companion, but because the young pastor's sickness had been the result of his overexposure in order to deliver good things to Paul, his death would have been to the apostle sorrow upon sorrow. God saved both Paul and Epaphroditus by healing him. We know that Epaphroditus was fully healed, because he was ready to make the return journey to Philippi.

8. An eighth objection to divine healing is that it puts more emphasis on the physical body than it does upon the soul and the spiritual experience. It is very possible that there are persons who desire divine physical healing only in order to be rid of disagreeable symptoms and to enjoy health for selfish reasons. The fact is that Jesus heals in order to show His love and mercy and to make us better servants of the Lord and of others.

Divine healing, being a part of our redemption, is given to complete our relationship to the Lord. He redeemed us soul and body; we also belong to Him soul and body. Paul wrote in 1 Corinthians 6:19, 20: "Or do you not know that your body is the temple of the Holy Spirit *who is* in you, whom you have from God, and you are not your own? For you were bought at a price; therefore glorify God in your body and in your spirit, which are God's." Divine health is glorifying to God in body.

Divine healing's purpose is spiritual; it is to draw us to our Lord. For instance, when the blind beggar, Bartimaeus, was healed of his blindness, if divine healing had been only to cure a malady, he would have gone home to see persons whom he had never seen, but instead he followed Jesus on His journey giving Him praise and glory (Luke 18:35–43). His healing did not release him to do his own thing; it liberated him to be a close follower of the Lord.

In the case of the woman who touched the hem of Jesus' garment, she had planned to touch Him secretly and to go away undetected. However, Jesus demanded immediately to know who had touched Him, forcing her to confess her act. Jesus wanted the woman to know the spiritual purpose behind His healing blessing. Jesus did not want the woman to think merely that she had obtained a *something*, He wanted her to know also that she received a part of Him; she came for *something* and got *Somebody*. Healing always establishes a relationship; if it does not, the healing may not endure.

Healing is a work of the Holy Spirit; it is not a magic touch or celestial pill. Healing sometimes requires confession of sin or the making right of an offense. Divine healing not only calls for a right relationship with others, it confirms our relationship with our Lord. It has been noticed that the majority of those who are gifted in praying for the sick are persons who have a healing testimony. Furthermore, healings are more abundant in an atmosphere of the Holy Spirit's strong presence.

9. A ninth objection is sometimes argued that the doctrine of healing is advanced only by the false cults. The fact is that the Lord intended that the full gospel should be a message of healing for soul and spirit. During the Dark Ages the church

fell into a spiritual decline during which spiritual results were meager. With the Protestant Reformation, there was a recovery of the gospel of justification by faith. However, while many were won to Christ, there was a minimum of teaching on the work of the Holy Spirit.

A few of the reformers, such as Zinzendorf and Wesley, restored teaching on healing, but it did not become a ministry of the church. In the vacuum, unorthodox teachings arose to appeal to the many sick people. It has been said that Satan takes truths the main body of the church neglects and distorts them for his purpose. If the church had obeyed the command of Jesus to "heal the sick," most of the healing cults would have found no ground of appeal. Most cult healing is not divine healing at all; it is "mind-over-matter," pantheistic philosophy; much of it is propounded in some present-day New Age teachings. But orthodox divine healing doctrine includes the fundamental teachings of the historic church, such as the finished atoning work of the Cross of Christ, including His virgin birth, His deity, His resurrection, His indwelling of the believer, the full work of the Holy Spirit and His return. Joined to these eternal verities, the ministry of healing is soundly based, and it is kept from the cultishly aberrant.

10. A tenth objection rises from those who reject the doctrine of healing in the Atonement, as prophesied by Isaiah. They explain away the passage in Matthew 8:16, 17 by arguing that the word "fulfilled" means that the cases of healing mentioned by that passage *completely* fulfilled Isaiah's prophecy: "He himself took our infirmities, and bore our sicknesses."

That this is an absurd theory is seen by several considerations:

(a) A few healings on one day in the life of Jesus could not fulfill a major prophecy such as that in Isaiah's great prophecy of the work of the Cross of Christ in Isaiah 53, where the healing statements are placed alongside the statements about the atonement for sin.

(b) If those few healings fulfilled Isaiah's prophecy, then there would not have been the thousands of healings that followed.

(c) If healing in the Atonement stopped with one group of healings, why would Peter later have said, "who Himself bore our sins in His own body on the tree, that we, having died to sins, might live for <u>righteousness—by whose stripes you were healed</u>" (1 Pet. 2:24)?

(d) If a few healings fulfilled Isaiah's whole prophecy about healing through the work of the Cross, how are we to be certain that all pardon for sin was not fulfilled by one conversion—say, of the Samaritan woman?

(e) A close look at the prophecy will show that it was not meant for a few sick in Galilee only, for it speaks of "<u>our</u> infirmities and <u>our</u> sicknesses." The word *our* makes the promise the timeless blessing for all of us to whom God's Spirit has given the Eternal Word.

(f) Finally, if we look at Matthew 12:17–21, where the word *fulfilled* is used, we will see that it can have reference to fulfillments that cover the whole church age. Has Jesus finished declaring justice to the Gentiles? Has He finished sending forth justice to victory? Has His name ceased being one in which the nations trust? Clearly not. A full study of the word *fulfilled* will show that the word means that what has happened is a beginning of what was prophesied.

11. Finally, let us look at an eleventh objection to healing: namely, that the doctrine of healing in the Atonement puts all believers who are not healed in a bad light. This is not necessarily true and never intentionally in the teaching. There are many reasons why some believers are not healed. A person may not have been healed because not all healings are instantaneous; in fact, many healings are gradual. Just as with salvation from sin, faith is the principal condition. Many very good Christians, especially those who have sat under teaching that cast doubt on the possibility of modern healing, will lack the positive faith to appropriate healing. And again, those who have been taught that sickness is the will of God for many people in order that they may be tested and tried, will have no faith for, or desire to pray for, deliverance, lest they pray contrary to God's will.

Although there is much spiritual reality beyond the average Christian's attainment, our goal should not be the average, but rather, the high calling of God in Christ Jesus (Phil. 3:12–15). Believe for God's highest!